bike tripping

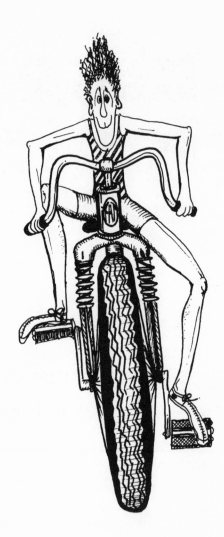

bike tripping

written by tom cuthbertson
illustrated by rick morrall

WITH A "FRAME" SECTION BY
ALBERT EISENTRAUT

BIKE TRIPPING is published
and distributed to the bike trade by
Ten Speed Press, Box 4310
Berkeley, California 94704

Distributed to the book trade by
Random House, and in Canada by
Random House of Canada, Ltd.

ISBN: 0-394-48150-X hardcover edition
0-394-70775-3 paperback edition

Library of Congress Catalog Card Number: 72-475

Typography: Beverly Anderson, San Francisco
First Printing, March 1972 3500 copies hardcover
50,000 copies paperback

Printed in the United States of America
by The Colonial Press, Clinton, Mass.

This book is dedicated
to Irving, the best dog in
the whole world, and
to my faithful Hetchins.

Acknowledgements

More than thanks to Pat and Al.
And thanks to these others among the many
who pitched in and/or tried to answer
my endless questions:
Paul Schoellhamer, Dan Nall, Roger Sands,
Peter Flanders, Ron Williams, Lynn Morrall,
Phil Shipley, Bill Muench, Gene Aybayani,
Al Kaiser, Peter Rich, and Mark Jansen

contents

Introduction

1 Learning To Ride 1

2 Which Bike For You 4

3 Safety and The Safe Bike 20

4 Hassle-less Town Cycling 31

5 Hassle-less Country Cycling 36

6 Transporting You and Your Bike 44

7 Tips For Happy Tripping 59

8 Getting On With The Elements 74

9 Local Bike Trips 85

10 Short Country Escape Routes 95

11 Tour Trips 102

12 The Road-Racing Trip 106

13 Bike Trips For The Fanatic Fringe 111

14 The Frame 125

Addresses 162

Appendix:

British Standard Wire Gauge Table . . . 164

Millimeter/Inch Conversion Table 165

Gear Table (27 Inch Wheel) 166

Index 169

T his is a book about how to have good trips on a bike. It can help you get into any facet of the cycling experience that might interest you, from cross country racing to urban commuting, from short "escape" trips around your neighborhood to long tours through the open countryside.

Many people are thinking about and talking about the cycling trip these days, not only because they are attracted by the sport itself, but also because they are getting turned off by other trips which have had their day and gone sour.

Take automobile tripping, for instance. We have all been having a mad love affair with the automobile since it took over the places of both the bicycle and the horse. We have saved the necessary pile of dough to buy a car, and the smaller piles of dough necessary to keep one going. We have polished and souped up our autos, then courted, honeymooned, and taken the family for Sunday drives in them. But we have gotten tired of cars. They are cramped with all the kiddies thrashing around in them. They make uncomfortable bedrooms. Their engines, we have learned, are hell-bent on self-destruction. They have turned the skies from blue to an ugly yellow-brownish color. And the cost of auto insurance has gotten to be absurd. So lately people have been searching for an alternative form of travel—a new trip.

Some have taken to jogging. It's a pretty basic and reliable way to get from place to place, and it's healthy, too. But it's a little slow if you want to get any change of scenery, and the constant bouncing up and down can rattle your brain after a while.

Some people have taken to drugs. Drugs give you a trip without your having to do anything. But with many drugs, you never know exactly what you are taking. And other people, like Feds, always try to find out what you are taking even if you aren't sure yourself. Besides, drugs often take your brain and body on scary trips to strange, lonely places. Like jails.

Some drop-outs from the car religion travel via mystic occult trips that take them to all sorts of extremes, while leaving them mostly in the same place.

But there is a growing number of people going back to that simple, reliable old means of mechanized transportation, the two-wheeler. Now, if you are trying the bike trip out, you'll know that it has its bummers, like any other escape from the humdrum. There are the flats, and the broken spokes, the pant cuffs caught in the chain, and the hassles with traffic and headwinds. But the great thing about bike riding is that you can always get through the difficulties if you are prepared for them, and move on to some new experience with a great feeling that you are doing something for yourself.

So the idea is first to help you minimize the problems of cycling, and second to introduce you to the many variegated good trips that can be had on bikes, trips that can not only keep you healthy and smog free, but also give you a new source of fun.

Ride out to the country. Expand your consciousness a little, and turn on to good old Mother Nature, before she starts turning on us.

The original trip on a bike doesn't have to be a bummer. If you take a few precautions, learning to ride a bike can actually be fun, and it can be done without scrapes, bruises, or even too much embarrassment.

Beginners should do their learning off the streets and highways. A perfect place to do any self-teaching, be it how to balance on a one speed, or how to shift a ten speed, is an empty parking lot, preferably one with a slight slope.

For those who have never ridden before, training wheels are an idea. But a better idea is to borrow a small bike (one that you can sit on with both feet touching the ground) and take it to your local slightly sloping parking lot. Learn to ride one step at a time, recapping the history of the bicycle as you learn. First try sitting on the bike and walking it along with your feet on either side. Then try coasting slowly, picking up your feet for short spaces, and putting them down to stop. That's the way the first bicycles worked, without pedals

Learning to ride on a small bike

or brakes. Learn how to operate the brakes on your bike, though, before you attempt coasting with any speed. If they are hand brakes, experiment and learn which brake is connected to which wheel. Make sure you use both brakes evenly at all times, right from the start. When you have coasting and braking down pat, learn to pedal and shift gears if you have more than one. Then you will be ready to get on the bike that's the right size for you.

If you are acquainting yourself with a ten speed, expect to spend some time coordinating your gear shifting technique. The gear system has no pre-set "position" for each gear, like a car's stick shift. Generally, though, moving the right lever forward puts you into a higher gear, as does pulling the left lever back. At first, your gears will gnash and skip as you shift, and rattle often between shifts. The derailleur, remember, will only shift when the chain is moving without tension. That means you have to move the pedals forward, but without putting pressure on them. If you are going uphill and want to shift to a lower gear, get up a little steam, then let off pressure on the pedals for just the amount of time it takes you to shift. Listen carefully after each shift. Your ears will tell you if the chain is seated properly. A silent chain is right where it should be. Usually, a ping-ping-ping noise indicates that the rear changer is about to move the chain to a lower gear than the one you wanted it to stay in—adjust by moving the right control lever forward slightly. A rapid clicking or whirring sound indicates that the chain is about to be moved to a higher gear on the freewheel. Pull back the right control lever slightly. Rubbing sounds indicate that the front changer cage is touching the chain. The higher pitched rubbing sounds mean that the outer side of the cage is hitting the chain. On most changers, you adjust by pulling back on the left control lever. Lower pitched rubbing sounds call for moving the left control lever forward a bit. Some front changers are now made in the opposite way. For these, obviously, the adjustments are the reverse.

Don't venture out of your peaceful parking lot training grounds until you have mastered your bicycle completely. And remember, when you do leave your sanctuary, you are going out into a cruel and indifferent realm of smogging two-ton monsters that you have to *watch* every minute. You can't be staring down at the bike to find the brake lever, or to see what gear you're in. Learn those things by heart so you can keep your full attention on the traffic.

2 WHICH BIKE FOR YOU

The second bike trip after learning to ride is picking the right bicycle for you. Many people had a bike or borrowed a bike and could ride when they were young. But for most of you now getting back into cycling, it's been some time since you rode much. While you may remember your good old balloon-tire Iverson, bikes and you have changed. So think a bit about today's bikes, and which type you're going to need.

First, do a little riding around to make sure you are up to the bike trip at all. Borrow a friend's one or three speed, or rent a one or three speed, and noodle around the block, the park, the neighborhood, or the farm, just to get back into the feel of what it was like in the good old days. You may be surprised by things like how hard it is to balance the bike at first, and how hard the seat is, and how much work it is to get a bike up a hill. Those things will all become easier as you move up to a light, multi-speed bike and get into better shape. Don't do your original "trying out" on a fancy ten speed though, especially if you've never ridden one before. Ten speed bikes, with the turned-down bars and the seat up in the air and all the complicated gismos down there moving the chain around are enough to alienate any beginner. It is only as you get deeper into the cycling trip that you begin to see the value of

One Speed

the specialized form and functions of the ten speed. So borrow a one or three speed. You should even consider buying that type of bike before you get onto a ten speed. So what if there's a fad on for ten speeds. The idea of cycling is to enjoy riding a bike, and if you aren't going to enjoy riding all folded up like a pretzel and straining your neck just to see where you're going, then get a one or three speed. They're a lot easier to come by than ten speed bikes these days, and a lot cheaper as well.

One and three speed bikes can be bought cheaply at discount stores and from catalogues. Often these bikes are either not assembled, or just thrown together in the store. In either case, you should sit down with the bike and a manual like the one I wrote, or some other aid, and go through the bike part by part, to make sure it is put together correctly and has all its nuts and bolts tightened up well. Handlebars, saddles, and wheels show especially strong tendencies toward looseness on new bikes. Be doubly sure your new bike seat isn't loose and misaligned.

If you're short on bread, you can find reliable transportation at flea markets, at garage or tag sales, at police auctions of stolen or lost bicycles, or in the want ads. A great alternative to a 20 pound bike with a 20 pound

Three Speed

lock and chain is a 40 pound "trashmo" special. Rick
the artist bought a used one speed for me at a flea market for five bucks. Works like a charm. And nobody
ever tries to steal it. For short around-town trips, commuting and shopping, or for school, the trashmo is the
only way to go. If you use a fancy bike for those trips,
you have to get a huge lock and chain, or get ulcers, or
both. Why not have two bikes—a trashmo for local
errands, and a super-bike for joy rides and longer trips.
Just make sure you tend to the maintenance needs of
your lovable old trashmo.

Several cuts above the trashmo bikes and the second
hand three speeds are the luxury three speed, four
speed, and five speed bikes. If you enjoy sitting upright,
and yet want a good, comfortable, reliable bike, look
at some of the elegant three speeds like the Raleigh
Superbe or the Moulton Collapsible Twenty (20 inch
wheel) or their counterparts in other makes. These
bikes are aristocrats. They are a joy to work on and
pure luxury to ride. The 20 inch wheel bikes are all
descendants or variations of the Moulton Four Speed,
a magnificent and now rare breed designed by Alex
Moulton of England. They look funny at first, like a
kid's bike with giraffe tendencies. Don't laugh. Some-
day they may take over. They are very comfortable,
especially those with built-in shock absorbers. They are
also amazingly maneuverable, and the collapsible models
are portable. You can take a fold-up Twenty on any

ONE 20 lb. BIKE

ONE 20 lb. LOCK

mass transit vehicle. In the future this may become increasingly important. So think twice before you turn down the idea of a three or four speed, 20 inch wheel bike in favor of the Walter Mitty dream you have of yourself on a racing bike.

Any serious bike, a three speed included, should be ridden before it is bought. Make sure you are getting the right size frame. On boys' bikes, the top tube of the frame should almost touch your crotch if you straddle the bike with both feet on the ground. It's harder to judge a girl's bike frame, because it has no top tube. Girls really have to sit on the bike to get an idea of the size. Get the shop to adjust the seat for you, whichever gender bike you are considering, then ride the bike around to make sure you like the feel of it. The difference between the feel of an inexpensive three speed and a Raleigh Superbe is immediately obvious. The difference between other bikes may be more subtle. Give them all a fair try, and don't let anyone tell you which one you should like. Including me. You may not dig that plushy ride of the Raleigh Superbe. Find out what *your* taste is.

Four and five speed bikes are a nice compromise between the upright position of the three speed bike and the wider gear range of the ten speed. They are usually made with the frame of the former, and some adaptation of gears from either a multi-speed hub or a ten speed type derailleur. They are fine for commut-

 ONE 40 lb. BIKE

Fold-up Twenty

ing and even longer jaunts, as long as you don't mind getting a little sore in the behind, and having to fight the wind a bit.

For the serious long-distance cyclist or the determined Walter Mitty, however, the lighter, more responsive ten speed bicycles are the way to go. You have to sacrifice the upright riding position, and get used to craning your neck to see where you're going, and learn how to manage all those gears, but in the long run, you'll find it's more than worth the trouble.

As far as the quality of different brands of ten speeds goes, only one thing is certain. Bikes change. There are established custom bike builders, like Masi or Cinelli of Italy, Singer or Herse of France, Jackson or Hetchins of England, as well as a number of others with whom I am unfamiliar. They all make and will probably continue to make bikes that are up to their high reputations. But even among those there are great differences and changes. Each builder makes different styles, too, and changes from year to year. Even if you know which custom bike you want, you might not be able to afford it.

The bikes most people can afford are production bikes. Mass produced. These fluctuate in quality. So don't just buy a name. Learn to look for things that make a good bike. You might refer to a bike like the Masi for comparison, just to get some kind of idea of a high standard of quality. But don't try to get a bike as much as possible like a Masi, or one with only Italian components like the Masi's—that may well be the wrong set-up for you. Just learn to compare the bikes in your price range, concentrating on whether each one *works the way you want it to.* Forget about which brand is "in" at the moment. Don't let yourself be sold on a bike by dealers or your friends. That's backwards. You are supposed to buy the bike you want, not get sold up the river.

If you are looking at the cheapest models of ten speed bikes (the price categories can't be given exact figures, because of inflation, trade wars, etc.), don't be too picky about things like the weight or liveliness of the bike and the quality of the finish. Look for cracks at any of the joints of the frame, though. Look closely at where the frame is brazed or welded to the fork

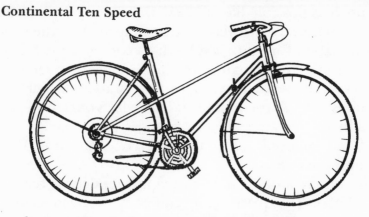

ends, too (the fork ends are the U-shaped slots into which the wheel axles fit). No new bike, no matter how inexpensive, should be coming apart at the seams.

Ask the dealer if he'll let you ride the bike. If he will, check to see that the gears and brakes work; don't expect flawless performance, but they should be functional. Try also to get a bike that's close to your size. You can adjust the seat at home, if the frame is nearly the right size. If the salesman won't let you ride the bike, at least pick up the wheels and give each a spin, listening to the bearings. If you hear or feel any grindy bearings, try to find a better bike for the money. On any inexpensive ten speed, it is essential to do the "tighten up and adjust everything" trip as soon as you get home. Get a nice repair manual and go through the Maintenance Check List carefully to become familiar with the bike's works, and learn what needs tightening and adjusting. Check the seat and handlebar bolts for sure. These are commonly loose on new bikes.

If you are shopping for a medium-priced ten speed, like one costing about one and a half to three times as much as the cheapest ten speed bikes, there are things that can be checked out to determine the comparative quality of the bike. Lift it up, for a start. Weight isn't the only factor in determining a bike's quality, but it is important if you plan to ride any distance at all, which you should, if you are going to put a sizable wad down for the bike. You'll get more fun for your money if you get less weight for your money, usually. The weight difference is insignificantly small in many comparisons, but you will discover that some bikes are notably overweight in comparison to the rest.

For a general idea of the quality of the workmanship in the bike, and the durability of it, look closely at the finish. Some bikes will have nice smooth joints, and good, hard paint jobs. Others will look sloppy at the lugs, and will have easy-to-chip soft paint. In most cases, the finish is a fair indication of the work beneath. While you're looking at the finish, don't be ashamed to take the color into consideration. Buy a bike that you like the looks of. You'll take better care of it, and it'll give you better service, even if it isn't quite up to the quality of the bike you thought was unattractive.

Ride the bike. Don't buy it if they won't let you ride it. And don't buy it unless you have good vibes about it after having ridden it. If the size seems funny, check the frame size. Stand astraddle the top tube with both feet flat on the ground. Your crotch should clear the top tube by about an inch. The seat should be at such a height that when you sit squarely on it and put a pedal at the bottom of its stroke, your leg extends fully and your foot rests flat on the pedal. The stem extension may not be adjusted quite right for you, and the seat may seem hard on that first ride, but other than that, you should like the feel of the bike. It should be a gut reaction. Ride. Like. Buy. If your feelings aren't that simple, take the thing for a longer ride. Ride over different pavement surfaces, up and down hills, and around sharp corners. The bike should be responsive, and feel lively as you go over bumps. Try riding no-handed a little, on a quiet street, if you can. The thing should go pretty straight by itself—that indicates a "true" frame, one which won't be working against you all the time. These criteria are all difficult to delineate, and impossible to objectivize. You are bound to have your own subjective interpretation of any criteria. That's fine. Just ride several different bikes, and learn to pick and choose by following the general guidelines set out above.

The gears and brakes on any medium-priced ten speed should work well, but if you have minor problems with either, like a chain throwing, or a brake shoe rubbing the rim, don't disqualify the whole bike. Any new bike has a few human errors and bugs in it; besides, new bikes and new riders take a while to get accustomed to each other. Don't go sour on a bike just because it has side-pull brakes, or a plastic derailleur, either. Both of these oft-maligned types of equipment often work better than their expensive relatives, especially if cared for well. And you want a bike that *works,* above all.

Think about the adaptability of the bike. Does it have little eyelets attached to the drop-outs, into which you can bolt carrier frames for grocery or luggage carrying, or fenders if you live where it rains a lot? Does the model you're looking at have low gears, like a small front sprocket with 44 teeth or less? If you plan to do any touring or steep mountain climbs, you'll want that low gear. Does the bike have sew-ups? There aren't many medium-priced bikes with sew-ups, but if you are looking at one, remember that although sew-ups make for an easier ride, and a lively feeling bike, they are easily punctured, and much more of a pain to repair than standard clincher tires.

If you are lucky enough to find a medium-priced bike with cotterless cranks, get the tool that fits them when you buy the bike, and tighten the cranks up once

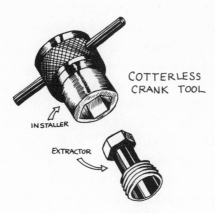

COTTERLESS
CRANK TOOL

INSTALLER

EXTRACTOR

every 25 miles for the first 250 miles. If you don't do
that, the cranks will come loose from the square end of
the axle, and the hard axle will dig into the soft alloy
cranks and ruin them.

Buy a good lock for the bike if you are ever going to
have to leave it for longer than about five seconds where
anyone might steal it. The best deal, according to a
scientific test made at Stanford University (see Addresses) is to buy a length of Campbell case-hardened
"cam-alloy" 9/32 inch thick chain, with a plastic tube
around it, and a strong padlock with a case-hardened
hasp. The whole outfit will weigh about two pounds.
It will guard the bike for shorter periods of time during
daylight. But don't rely on any lock too heavily. Remember the maxim, "No lock is better than the human
eye." Take your bike inside with you whenever it's
possible, or keep it locked outside a window you can
keep glancing through. Never leave the bike outside at
night, no matter what kind of lock you have on it.
Space age thieves can get through any lock or chain,
given a little time.

If you plan to get an expensive ten speed, that is to
say, one that costs from five to eight times as much as

the cheapest models, bone up before you pay out. Ride on a decent bike until you know what kind of bike trip you like, and how strong you are, and what particular "feel" you favor in a bike. Then read Al Eisentraut's beautiful chapter. Twice. And think about it all for a while. You don't want to make a foolish or half-educated decision if you are going to be spending 400 clams or more. If you feel dwarfed, as I do, by all the technical knowledge that goes into frame-building, and if you'd rather rely on someone who is likely to know what you want better than you, order a custom frame. Tell the dealer, or better yet, write to the frame maker himself and tell him your size (see the picture for the necessary measurements), what sort of cycling you will do, and generally what sort of frame, limber or stiff, you prefer. You can trust a custom frame maker like Al Eisentraut. His business is to design the bike to fit your needs.

If you can't afford that ideal route, learn a little from Al about frame design and alignment, and what makes for differences in stiffness and limberness in a frame. Then take a measuring tape, your educated eye, and (if you want to check alignment) some string, dividers, and a straightedge, and go to a shop looking for the design best suited to your needs. For instance, if you are heavy, and very strong, and tend to have a brutal or choppy riding style, and think you might go in for short races or criterium racing, you'll do best with a stiff, relatively short bike. If you are lighter, and a smoother-styled cyclist, one who likes long rides and expects to cover some territory with rough road surfaces, you should try the limber bikes.

If you have more complicated needs than those two simple examples, think carefully about what design of bike will produce the ride you want. Read Al's chapter again, and try to find out as many things as possible about any bikes you are considering. Talk to racers who have ridden the bikes. Learn the reputation of a bike before you buy.

Think about the wheels as well as the frame. Wheels can play a significant role in a bike's ride, and in its durability. If they have high-flange hubs, four-crossed spokes (spokes laced in such a way that each one intersects four others between hub and rim) which are wire-tied and soldered at the outer intersection, they are going to be very stable. Good for smooth track racing. You have to pay for the stability though. On wheels with high-flange hubs and four-crossed spokes, the spokes enter the rim at an angle, instead of perpendicular to the tangent. This angle expresses itself, in time, as a bend in the spoke at the point where it enters the nipple. The spokes tend to break at that point. If you want more resilient, durable wheels, ones which will absorb road shocks instead of telegraphing them to the frame and you, get ones with good low-flange hubs (there are some very fine American sealed-bearing hubs being made these days, and sealed bottom bracket sets are coming soon; kudos to Phil Wood). Three-crossed spokes are fine, laced or woven so they touch at the outer intersection for a little extra rigidity. A fine wheel should be equipped with a good, resilient rim like the Scheeren, with its wood insets, or any other rim with ferrules reinforcing the spoke holes. Get wheels with butted stainless steel, or rustless spokes too. Not only are they shiny and lightweight; they are less vulnerable to fatigue and rust. For extra strength in the rear wheel, get one with 40 spokes, and maybe even a heavier than normal rim.

Of course, you should check for trueness of the wheels by spinning each, and watching the rim where it passes between the brake shoes. But remember, a slight rim wobble can be adjusted away.

It is more important to check the trueness of the bike's frame. Stand in front of the bike and line up the head tube with the seat tube by sighting along their right edges. The edges should be exactly parallel. For another test, put your head down between the chainwheels and the front wheel. Sight between the chainwheels back to the freewheel. The middle sprocket on the freewheel should appear in the narrow space between the chainwheels. See Al's chapter for other checks you can make.

The other equipment on the expensive bike will probably be of very high quality and up to your needs even if it isn't all made by that famous Italian company. But you might notice differences in performance, like in brakes for instance. Center-pull brakes have very good leverage, but some brands tend to get sticky. Side-pull brakes are simpler, a little lighter, and some brands are designed so that they have leverage almost as positive as that of the center-pull brakes. Try all the different types for yourself, but don't be too disappointed if your favorite isn't available on a particular bike. Any decent brake system will stop the bike adequately if used properly (see "How to Ride Wisely").

A word about gears. Too much fuss is made over them. For serious road racing on anything but steep hills, the smooth progression of sprockets on the freewheel with the following numbers of teeth is best: 14-16-18-20-22. The 13-21 set is OK, but the 13 tooth sprocket will tend to wear out quickly. For extremely hilly racing, or long-distance riding, or even touring, the wider-ranged smooth progression of 14-17-20-23-26 is quite satisfactory. If you race strong, but expect some steep hills, a compromise is the 14-16-18-21-24 set. Other combinations, with huge low gear sprockets, 13 tooth small sprockets, and all kinds of uneven progressions in between are bad for the changer, your pace, and your performance. The same is true of chainwheels. A 36-58 combination not only out-ranges most rear changers' ability to take up slack chain—it also forces the cyclist to do all kinds of weird pacing. A 44-52 set, a 46-54 set, or for touring, a 40-50 set will do everything any able rider needs. Even closer ranges than the former ones might be better for certain races. That's up to the rider.

As for the talk about how many "inches" any particular gear is, the inches refer to the size wheel any particular gear would require if it were straight drive. A 54 inch gear does not mean that the bike travels 54 inches forward for each revolution of the cranks. It means that if the pedals were attached directly to a wheel, that wheel would have a 54 inch diameter. Remember the high-wheelers? Many of them had a 54 inch gear. The 54 inches in terms of modern bikes is arrived at by a simple formula:

$$\frac{\text{NO. OF TEETH ON FRONT SPROCKET}}{\text{NO. OF TEETH ON REAR SPROCKET}} \times 27 \text{ INCHES}$$

So, for a 54 inch gear, you could have a 48 tooth front sprocket and a 24 tooth rear, or a 52 tooth front and a 26 tooth rear. A two-to-one ratio, in other words. With a 52 tooth front sprocket and a 14 tooth rear, you have a 100 inch gear. A direct drive wheel would be 100 inches in diameter. WOW! You'd have to wear stilts to reach the pedals on a high-wheeler made with a wheel that big. If you want to figure out how many inches your gears are, so you can put all the combinations in progression, and write them on a little tape and stick it to your stem extension, you can count all the teeth and do the math with your greasy fingers, or use the gear chart in the back of this book, getting it all greasy in the process. But wouldn't you be spending all that time and energy more wisely by riding the bike? You will

develop your own gear shifting tactics with long practice. You can't short-cut the process by doing a little
paper work.

Back to the bike. As for gear changers on new bikes,
get the one that will do the job you want it to. Some
of the best changers are designed for racers who use a
narrow range of gears on the freewheel, like the 14-22
tooth set. If you want to use a wider range of gears,
you may find the well-known super-changer inadequate.
Try the top-of-the-line model that's made out of plastic
and spring steel. You think plastic has no place on a
fancy derailleur? Take another look at the chain rollers
on the later models of the well-known super-changer.
My, my. A second alternative to the plastic changer for
wide range is the awkward looking, but extremely
smooth aluminum alloy model from the mystic east.
The idea is to shop around before you buy the most
expensive changer, unless you road-race with close
ratio. For that, there's nothing much better than the
Italian super-changer with its super-price.

Any expensive bike is likely to have cotterless
cranks. Lately, even most track racers use them. Get
the crank tool that fits your cranks and tighten them
up every 25 miles for the first 250. The seat that comes
with the bike is bound to be good, but in the great
leather vs. leather-covered nylon seat debate, I'm afraid
I am about to go back to good old English leather after
a long trial of the competition. For long distance riders,
if you have a strong, top-grade butt leather seat that
you have been using for a while, keep it for any new
bike. It fits you, and that puts it way above any other
seat in value.

There are no systems for adjusting the seat and handlebar positions that cover all the different possibilities
of rider size, strength, and riding style. Experiment.

Find the combination of positions that is comfortable for you. Keep the seat close to level though, and keep it at a height where it neither over-stretches nor cramps your legs. The handlebars should be close to level on top, too, through the first bend, unless they are track bars. Road bars should have a stem extension that allows you to use several different hand positions comfortably.

Whatever expensive bike you start getting seriously interested in, ride it before you buy it. Fill the tires to the proper pressure, and ride the bike extensively, and hard. Ride it no-handed. It should go straight by itself, even if it is a short, stiff frame. If you are experienced at all, which you should be if you're about to get an expensive bike, you'll know pretty soon if the bike you're testing is what you want.

When you finally make your decision, and buy the bike, don't ride it downtown and leave it outside the market with a cable lock holding it to a parking meter. No lock is really sufficient for that kind of bike, unless the weakest link is of half-inch thick case-hardened steel, which makes for a ridiculous amount of dead weight. Take the bike with you wherever you go, or leave a trusty friend watching it. At night, if you can't keep it in the same room, lock it to a pipe with a Campbell case-hardened 7/16 inch chain and a padlock of complementary proportions. This will give you the best odds, according to an independent study of locks and chains (see Addresses).

3 SAFETY AND THE SAFE BIKE

A bicycle is such a wonderfully maneuverable machine that it tends to give the cyclist a feeling of freedom and complete security, once he has learned to ride it well. But alas, the very things which make the bicycle so maneuverable, like its lightness and compactness, are the things which make it vulnerable in traffic. Too many cyclists are being injured these days. Bicycle riders should always expect to take an occasional spill, but the injuries from such spills are usually minor, whereas any collision between a car and a bike is extremely traumatic for the cyclist. The point is, when you are sharing the road with something ten times bigger and heavier than you, *WATCH OUT!*

Bike riders are in a very small, though growing, minority group. As a cyclist, you don't own the road, and you can't push the big guys on it around, because they can run you over. Splat. That easily.

THE BASIC SAFETY LAW

Most state Vehicle Codes don't say much about bikes. Bikes are often ignored, or left to local control, as in Texas, where you might cross a county line or a city limit, and find yourself under totally different

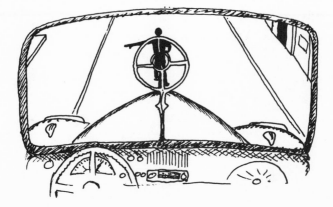

Illegal Bike

restrictions. When there are state laws governing bikes, they are often of little value to the everyday cyclist. For instance, a law which crops up in a fair number of the Vehicle Codes is one which stipulates that no bike can have pedals that are more than twelve inches above the ground (?!). There is one valuable basic law, however, in almost every state, which must be followed. It usually reads something like:

Every person riding a bicycle upon a roadway has all the rights and is subject to all the duties applicable to a driver of a vehicle.

In other states, the bicycle is "deemed a vehicle, and must therefore conform to traffic rules and regulations, so far as they are obviously and reasonably applicable." Either law means the same thing. No running stop signs and lights, no erratic weaving and swooping through traffic, no turning without hand signals, no riding on crowded sidewalks, no riding three abreast and blocking the flow of traffic. OK? That isn't too much to ask.

So DO IT. Stay alive and in one piece. There's so much cycling to be done, and you can't do it if you have to wear a cast all the time.

As for night riding, no matter what your state or local government has to say about it, it is spooky, isn't it? Sometimes it can be fun, like on a deserted country road in the moonlight, but it can be awful when you get blinded by headlights, then run into a chuckhole, then pop your tire on some glass you never saw. Cycle at night only when you have to. If you are cycling for pleasure, stick to the daylight hours, and be careful

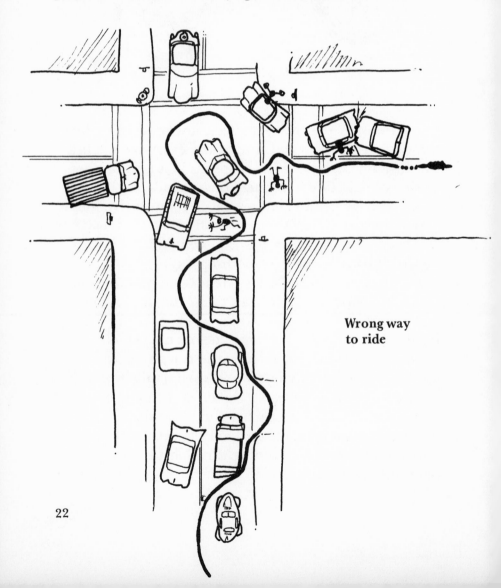

**Wrong way
to ride**

even before sunset, because the low sun can blind drivers so they don't see you. If you have to ride at night, by all means use a light. Most people emphasize the front light, and make sure they have a nice big chrome-plated one, even though no bicycle light made will light up the road adequately. People often neglect to get a good taillight, or even a reflector. The greatest danger for the night cyclist is someone clobbering him from behind without ever seeing him. So get a good taillight as well as a reflector. State Vehicle Codes usually require something like the following:

Every bicycle operated upon any highway during darkness shall be equipped with a lamp emitting a white light visible from a distance of 300 feet in front of the bicycle and a red reflector on the rear of a type approved by the department which shall be visible from a distance of 300 feet to the rear when directly in front of lawful upper beams of headlamps on a motor vehicle. A lamp emitting a red light visible from 300 feet to the rear may be used in addition to the red reflector.

Lately, many states have added a new requirement that reads something like

No person shall sell a new bicycle or pedal for use on a bicycle that is not equipped with a reflector, of a type approved by the department, on each pedal of such bicycle which is visible from the front and rear of the bicycle during darkness from a distance of 200 feet.

All that strange language is trying to say one thing. You need a good light *and* a good reflector for night riding.

The best solution to the light problem is the French-designed armband light. It is nothing more than a little flashlight with a single bulb and two lenses, a clear one that faces forward, and a red one that faces the rear. The red lens is also a reflector, so that even if your batteries run out, you still give warning to cars coming up from behind. Wear the French light on your leg, just below your knee, instead of on your arm. It fits naturally there, and stays in place if you tighten the strap well and then tie it in a knot. As you pedal, the light will bob up and down, so that motorists can't possibly miss it. The idea of reflectors on the pedals, as presented in the new law, is good, and tries to serve the same purpose as the bobbing French light. But reflectors on pedals tend to break, get covered with mud, or be hidden by your heels. So don't rely on pedal reflectors. Spend the measly two clams or whatever for the French armband light, and save your life by strapping it on your leg for all night riding.

In some states, there are laws which require all lights and reflectors to be stationary and fixed to vehicles. This law seems to confute the new pedal-reflector law. If you are in doubt, put a reflector on the back of your bike, like under the seat, and use the French light on your leg as well. If that still upsets the police, you have to sacrifice the bobbing light (some police think the bobbing light looks too much like an emergency vehicle light) and put the armband light on your arm. So far, I haven't been bothered by the gendarmes for using mine on my leg. I hope it stays that way.

Safe riding in the dark takes some know-how as well as a good taillight. If you have to ride at night often, like to and from work or school, develop a regular route through the least possible amount of traffic and obstacles. Then stick to that route, keeping an eye out for things like glass or chuckholes that crop up occasionally. If you ride in the city at night, stick to lighted streets, and don't take short-cuts through creepy parks, just as you wouldn't if walking. If you live in the country, and ride on straight, dark farm roads, you can watch for car

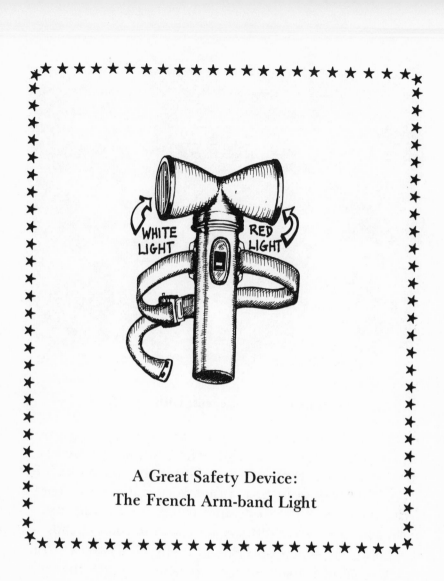

WHITE LIGHT

RED LIGHT

A Great Safety Device:
The French Arm-band Light

lights coming up behind you by looking down at the rim of your front wheel. The headlights' reflection can be seen in the shiny rim long before you hear the car or see its light coming up beside you.

When you come to an interesection or a blind corner at night, either in the city or the country, watch for the glare of headlights of cars that might be approaching from around the corner. When you are riding directly

Motorist's view of cyclist without light

at an on-coming car on a straight road, look down at
the edge of the road to your right, and close your left
eye. That way your nose (especially if it's a big nose)
will shade your right eye, and when the car goes by,
you can open your left eye and see the road ahead.

Above all, when you ride at night, ride slowly. You
are bound to hit some road obstacles at night that you
would miss in the daylight. The slower you are going,
the less damage an obstacle will cause.

THE SAFE BIKE

A safe bike is a well-maintained bike. For a pretty
good list of things to keep an eye on, you can look at
the Maintenance Checklist in the repair manual I wrote.
For those of you who can't get that book, here's an
abbreviated version of the list.

Check your wheels, to make sure that the big axle nuts, wing nuts, or quick release levers that hold the wheels to the frame are good and tight.

Check your tires for wear, and check the air pressure in them. They should say what the recommended pressure is on the wall somewhere, and you can check with a tire gauge. But a simple and reliable spot check can be done as well. Take the bike to a curb or stair, put the wheel on the edge of it, and push down from above (see illustration). The edge of the curb should push into the tire easily, so that the sides of the tire squish out visibly; but the edge of the curb shouldn't squish the tire all the way so that you can feel the rim knock the curb. Sew-up tires, like on racing bikes, should be so hard that a good heavy shove from above is needed to squish the tire out at all. But be careful, with any tire, if you are filling it at a gas station. Gas station pumps can even pop most sew-ups.

Make sure the tire valve always comes straight through the rim on whichever kind of tire you have. On sew-ups, a crooked valve means the whole tire has to be taken off and re-glued to the rim. To straighten a clincher, let all the air out, then start at the valve and work away from it all the way around the tire,

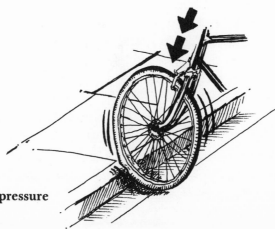

Testing tire pressure

pinching the beads of the tire together, pulling them away from the rim, and then moving the tire a bit at a time. Do the pinching and pulling with one hand, and hold the wheel still with the other.

Check the brakes on the bike, especially if they are hand brakes. Hand brakes should be adjusted so that the end of the hand lever travels about two inches to fully apply the brake. Make sure the rubber shoes are aligned so that they hit the wheel rim squarely.

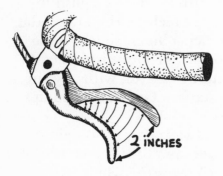

Brake lever travel

Handlebar stem

Check the seat post and the handlebar stem, to make sure that at least two inches of the length of each is stuck down into the bike frame. To check the seat post, loosen the binderbolt (the bolt that squeezes the bike frame around the post), then pull the seat up to make sure two inches were down in the frame. To check the handlebar stem, loosen the expander bolt (the bolt whose hexagonal head sticks up out of the top of the back of the stem) about two turns. Then tap the head of the bolt with a hammer. This will loosen the stem so you can pull it out and see how much was down in the frame.

Check your gears, if you have more than one, and make sure their range is adjusted properly. On a three speed, this means putting the bike in the middle gear and going to the right side of the back wheel and finding the little chain that disappears into the center of the wheel. This is the indicator. When the bike is in the middle gear, the indicator should be adjusted so that you can look through that little hole in the side of the long pole-shaped axle nut that the indicator goes through, and see the place where the indicator chain is attached to a smooth pole, which goes into the axle. (If you have one of those Japanese three speeds, there's often an arrow with an "N" to make things simpler.) To get a better look at the smooth indicator pole, shift to a low gear. Look through the hole in the side of the axle nut. See the smooth pole? Good. Now shift back to the middle gear. Adjust the indicator by tightening or loosening the adjustable sleeve which attaches the indicator to the cable going up to the control lever that's on the handlebars. When the sleeve is adjusted correctly, tighten the little knurled locknut that's around the indicator against the adjustable sleeve.

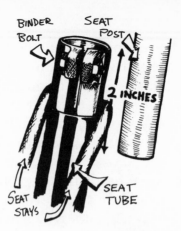

Seat post

For ten speed people, adjusting the range of the
gear-changing mechanisms is more complicated. It involves adjusting the range-limiting screws. Get someone
to teach you how to do this well, or learn how to do
it from *Anybody's Bike Book*. But learn how to do it
well, and KEEP AFTER IT. A poorly adjusted derailleur
can mean a ruined rear wheel, a smashed gear changer,
and a bad accident.

Check your pedals where they are screwed into the
cranks, especially on new bikes. Pedals don't make any
warning noises when they are coming loose. Most other
parts of the bike will tell you when they need attention, but the pedals can unscrew soundlessly.

Check your chain and make sure it is covered with
a fine film of fine oil, like 3-in-1, or better, LPS 3 chain
lubricant. A dry chain tends to slip and throw.

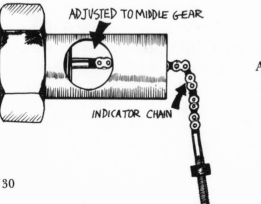

Adjusted three speed

4 HASSLE-LESS TOWN CYCLING

Getting around on a bike in town takes more than obedience to the scant laws and the use of a well-maintained bike. Towns are the automobile's turf. Cyclists should ride with all due respect, and only try to beat cars on their own turf when they are stopped dead still. Even then the bike rider has to watch out for the seemingly magical appearance of nightmarish enemies. A parked car's door can swing out at him, for instance; a slatted grate might yawn open under his front wheel; a two-ton mountain of glittering chrome leaps out of a driveway. And the whole scene is played out to the tune of honking horns, roaring engines, and the cursing of impatient drivers.

The first rule for the cyclist riding in city traffic is: *AVOID THE TRAFFIC*. Find routes that take you where you want to go without using the main thoroughfares. See the chapter on Local Trips for some hints. If your town is nice enough to provide bike trails, find out where they are from the Chamber of Commerce, a bike club, or the local bike shops, and use the trails whenever possible. Use back streets that run parallel to the main streets. Steer clear of one-way, rapid traffic routes with no room at the sides for cyclists. Streets with parked cars along them, hazardous as they are, still usually have more room for you than the streets with moving traffic curb-to-curb. Cut across parks and empty parking lots when it is allowed. On narrow bridges, use the sidewalk if there is one, and in residential areas, use the footpaths. If you follow the same route every day, perfect it; change it if it needs changing to make it safer. If you want to take a pleasure ride, in town or in the suburbs, do it early on a weekend morning. You'll be amazed at how little traffic there is from seven to eleven on Saturday and Sunday. Sound early? It is, but it's well worth the trouble.

Most bicycle accidents in town occur at intersections. So, obviously, you must *BE SUPER CAREFUL AT INTERSECTIONS.* Remember that the cars aren't looking for you. *You* have to watch out for *them.* Watch especially for people making left-hand turns, and people coming up from behind you, passing you, and then making right-hand turns right into you. The motorist making a right-hand turn is always looking to the left, watching for cross-traffic. He's not going to be aware of you, even if you are only a foot away from his car. Buses pulling in and out of stops at intersections are a similar problem. Stay clear of them, even if it means taking to the sidewalk or a traffic lane. Taxis should be given plenty of room, too. In some cities, like New York, cabbies seem to take delight in terrorizing bike riders.

The worst way to enter an intersection is to come flying off a curb at full speed, and shoot out through the traffic. That's *asking* for trouble. In busy intersections, unless you are an experienced rider, you are best off walking the bike across the crosswalk. If you want to ride through, and can stay close to the speed of the traffic, ride in a traffic lane where you will be seen by cars. Let a car run interference for you. As you slow down coming towards the intersection, find a car that is going the same direction as you through it, and follow along ten feet behind him. This is especially helpful if you want to make a left turn. Keep your hands on your brakes, though, and be ready for your "blocker" to stop.

No matter where you ride in town, the law makes it clear as to which side of the road you are supposed to use. *KEEP TO THE RIGHT.* The law sometimes reads: "Every person operating a bicycle upon a roadway shall

ride as near the right side of the roadway as practicable, exercising care when passing a standing vehicle or one proceeding in the same direction." The law is a good one. Many states don't make it so clear, but the idea is that you are in a much better position to see and be seen by motorists if you stick to the right side of the road. And as is suggested, you must be especially cautious when passing parked cars, or cars moving slowly. In a traffic jam, as you pass a whole string of backed-up cars, be on the lookout for some impatient guy who might suddenly pull out of the line in front of you.

When passing a whole row of parked cars, look *into* the cars for drivers who might open their doors or pull out suddenly in front of you. If you want to be doubly cautious, you can look not only at and in parked cars, but also *under* them for little legs and feet of children and pets who might dash out as you approach. If you ride on quiet side streets, or quiet four-lane streets, you can avoid many of the parked car hazards by riding five or six feet out towards the middle of the street. Is it legal to ride out there in the traffic lane? A good question. If a policeman stops you, you can quote your faithful law, as was quoted above, and tell him that it is not "practicable" to ride right next to parked cars with their many hazards. Keep in mind, though, that you must not hold up a line of cars behind you at any time. Vehicle Codes have either some provision which

reads like, "a slow-moving vehicle, behind which five
or more vehicles are formed in line, shall turn off the
roadway at the nearest place designated," or a law for-
bidding the impedance of the "normal flow of traffic."
Remember the maxim that you can't push the big guys
around, because they can run you over. Splat. Like that.
Be polite. Pull over and let cars pass you. Keep a low
profile.

You can sometimes tell whether cars are behind you
by listening, but with the noise levels in towns going up
the way they are, you can't always depend on your ears.
Learn to glance around to your left quickly, without
swerving or taking your attention off the road ahead
for more than half a second. It takes some practice, but
put some time into that quick glance to the rear until
you are adept at it. It'll save your bike and body. If
only cyclists had panavision eyes like frogs, or two pro-
files, that would simplify things. If you wear glasses or
a cap when you ride, you can get a nifty little rear-view
mirror that clips onto them. The mirror, a Chuck Harris
invention, works amazingly well, though it doesn't give
you a full view of what's behind you (see Addresses).

As for the normal city hazards like slatted drain
grates or streetcar tracks, always steer clear of them, or
if you have to cross them do so at right angles
to the cracks your
wheels want to
fall into.

5 HASSLE-LESS COUNTRY CYCLING

Riding out in the country is often a better trip than town cycling, especially if you use lesser-traveled roads like those shown on the Country Trips maps in this book. Such roads are quiet all day in many places. There is less competition for the cyclist to worry about. But you still have to keep your eyes and ears open for traffic. To stay out of the traffic's way, keep well to the right, especially in blind curves. It's funny how often the only two cars you will see on some lonely road are two cars that come on you simultaneously from opposite directions in a blind curve. If you always ride over to the right side of the road, you can glance over your left shoulder to keep an eye on the cars coming up from behind. At the same time, though, be careful not to ride off the edge of the pavement onto a soft shoulder or into a ditch. That can be embarrassing. If you ride a balloon-tire bike, keeping off the pavement all the time is best, but for thin-tired bikes the shoulder is usually too soft.

Be on the lookout for hazards like cattle guards and tracks. These should be crossed at a fair clip (ten to fifteen miles per hour) and in such a way that your direction of travel is exactly perpendicular to the rails or bars. Never cross a cattle guard or railroad tracks, especially wet ones, diagonally.

On downhill runs the obvious danger is speed. Maybe you like going fast down hills, but try to control your urge to zoom when you are unfamiliar with the curves. Also keep the momentum down on any roads where you even suspect big chuckholes, which can cause wheel damage, or patches of gravel, which invite skids. You may notice that gravel and chuckholes are most common in the middle of hairpin turns. This is because sharp corners are often cut into hillsides, so that gravel falls onto the road. Also, cars always slam on their brakes going through sharp corners, creating that "washboard" effect of ripply pavement and eventually lots of chuckholes. So approach blind, sharp curves with extra caution. When you are going fast through any blind curve, by the way, *keep well to the right.* Cars often cut sharp corners—you don't want to meet them head-on in the middle.

Wet roads are slippery. Ride slowly in the rain, on the level as well as downhill. Look far ahead for any trouble coming up, so if you have to slow down you can apply your brakes very gently for a few seconds to dry them off, then put them on hard to slow or stop. Wet brakes on a slick, wet road can be nightmarish.

Less of a danger than wet roads, but almost as bothersome, are freshly tarred and graveled country roads. *Don't* ride on them. If you do by mistake, you can get

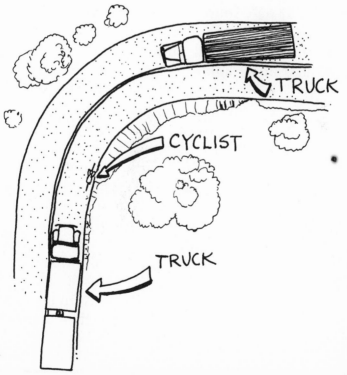

TRUCK

CYCLIST

TRUCK

the resultant layer of goo off your tires with turpentine on a rag. Try to keep the turpentine off the gum walls of fancy tires, though; it eats into them.

There are various animals the country rider must watch out for. Deer, raccoon, skunks, opossums, and cattle (though they're pretty dumb and stampede-prone) will get out of your way if you give them half a chance. Make a wide berth around deer; a startled deer can bolt in an unexpected direction.

Cats and dogs are another story. For cats, you should slow down, and don't be surprised if they suddenly shoot across the road in front of you. They tend to leave the safe edge of the road and dart out just as danger approaches.

Dogs. Ah, yes, dogs. Sometimes they make you wish you had those weapons like the charioteers used in Ben-Hur, with the knives that came spinning out of the wheel hubs, slashing the competition to bits. Short of that sort of ugly solution to the dog problem, there is no one simple answer. You should be ready to do different things depending on whether you are going downhill, flat, or uphill.

If you are going downhill, slow as you approach a barking or threatening dog, and try to figure out whether he is going to run at you or not. If he doesn't, give him a wide berth, pass slowly, and ride on at a good clip. You'll probably be able to outrun him if he should give chase. If a dog looks hell-bent on doing you in, slow down, try to keep your nerve and hold a straight course, then just hope that the bugger has good enough judgment to stop his charge before you hit him. Ninety-nine cases out of a hundred he will. For the hundredth time, see "Just in Case." Otherwise, when the dog stops coming at you, take advantage of his momentary imbalance and pedal like hell on down the hill.

BEN HUR
HUB

If you are riding on level ground and approach a threatening dog, gauge your strength against his potential speed. If he's an Irish wolfhound with blood dripping from his fangs, for instance, try to make friends, or lie down and play possum, or change your course 180 degrees. If the dog is small and slow-looking, you can use the downhill approach. Hold a straight course and outrun him.

Going uphill, you can't outrun most dogs unless you are a racer or so scared that your adrenaline is making you as strong as a racer. If you confront a dog that looks like he wants to do more than bark at you, try to figure out what will discourage him. No one method will work with all dogs.

A good firm "No!" accompanied by a shaking finger or pump is a fair starter. If that doesn't work, you have to decide quickly to either a) turn around and high tail it back down the hill; b) pull a Gandhi special by dropping the bike and lying down or making peace in some way; or c) employ some escalated form of finger-pointing.

If you can conveniently change your route by heading down the hill, that's the easiest out. Or, if you can calm the dog by going across the road and passing him slowly, talking soothingly, that's fine too. Often, the reason for a dog's anger is that you are entering his territory. A dog that wanders a bit from home, then turns to find you blocking him from the safety of his home front is an angry dog. Give way, and let him get on the home side of you, and he may become a barker instead of a biter.

If you seem bound unavoidably for attack, the Gandhi, or play-possum trick is great, providing you have the guts. I've seen a vicious German shepherd turn into a sniffing, confused, and silly-looking victor over a supine cyclist. A variation on the theme is to hop off the opposite side of the bike from the dog, crouch down low, and say "No," firmly, but not excitedly (good luck on keeping your cool). The idea in either approach is to get down from your towering height above the dog. Dogs, like many other animals, relate a raised figure with a challenge. Seals raise their heads up as high as possible when they want to challenge an opponent. Gorillas get up on their hind legs. Cats and dogs raise their heads, tails, and hackles. People get up on soap boxes or summit conferences. When a dog sees you looming up, a tall, over-bearing violator of his territory, by god, you pose a challenge. If you dismount and lower yourself and look him in the eye and say "No," you become something more like a master than a challenger. The dog will probably go right on

180° change in course

barking, out of confusion if nothing else, but he won't
be as likely to attack.

If you want to escalate from the finger-pointing
technique, you can choose your weapon from a vast
and ingenious arsenal. Use a squirt gun with a little
ammonia in water. Use your hand pump. Use an electric cattle prod, if you're the mechanized cow-puncher
type. But try to get by with *pointing* your weapon and
saying "No" before you injure a dog and teach it to
hate cyclists more than it already does. Any form of
weapon used against a dog has a built-in risk of escalat-
ing his attack. And a really furious dog, even a relatively
small one, can hurt you badly, no matter what you try
to stop him with. So from a practical as well as a philosophical standpoint, avoidance and conciliation are
better than out-and-out war.

Try not to hate dogs, even if one does bite you or
cause you to spill after you have used the above methods of avoidance. Hating dogs, swearing vengeance on

them, will help nothing. If you yell and scream and attack every vaguely defensive dog you come across, you are going to make a lot of canine enemies for the rest of the cycling world. Dogs should learn to accept cyclists as something bigger than they are, but not as something to be fought to the death.

Another animal which can give the country cyclist trouble is the homo sapiens, especially those who go out to the country to avoid the police. When you are gliding along a silent, deserted country lane, keep your ears open for sounds like roaring engines and squealing tires, or gunshots. Unfortunately, people take to the peaceful country to do things like get drunk and drag race, or do a little illegal pot-shooting. When you hear approaching hot-rodders, prepare to leave the road. When you hear gunshots, stay on the road, and try to keep up a stiff pace. Believe it or not, gun-nuts sometimes think cyclists make neato moving targets, especially if there isn't anything else around to shoot at.

The more decent legal hunters are to be considered, too. Riding on lonely dirt roads in beige outfits during the deer season is sheer idiocy. Wear bright orange, and stick to paved, public access roads during the hunting season. The vast majority of the legal hunters are nice, and respectful of cyclists; they seem to be out in the country for many of the same reasons you are—escape from work and town, and a chance to breathe fresh air and get into their own nature trip. If you come across a hunter, keep quiet, so you don't scare any wildlife, and try to keep the peace with him. If hunters learn to dislike cyclists, they might take to pot-shotting like their illegal gun-nut counterparts.

Sometimes, while riding in the open country, especially on long trips, you will be tempted to use a limited access, high-speed road. The law usually prohibits cycling on freeways. Obey it. Even if your state allows riding on freeways or high-speed toll roads, pretend there is a law prohibiting it. There are good reasons for such a law. The construction of freeways and the speed of the vehicles traveling on them are totally antithetical to cycling.

If you are planning a long trip, get good maps, like the U.S. Geological Survey Topographic maps (see Addresses), or AAA maps, and search out routes that avoid the freeways. If there is no way around a freeway shown on a map, ask the locals when you get there. Sometimes gas station attendants and farmers know ways to get around the freeways. They use little-known routes for transporting farm equipment. If there is simply no alternative to the freeway, hitch a ride with a car or truck; anything is better than riding on the nasty concrete no-man's land with cars going by you at 70 plus.

6 TRANSPORTING YOU AND YOUR BIKE

The best way in the world to transport your bike is to pedal it, or, if a hill is too steep, push it along. But modern life is not designed around the cyclist. Sometimes you will have to move yourself and your bike over great distances in short amounts of time. The most ecological way to do this is via some form of public transportation. But if no mass transit is available, you have to get there by attaching the bike to a car.

PUBLIC TRANSPORTATION

Public transportation is at a low ebb right now, but it will undoubtably become much more important in the future. Imagine the day when you will pedal down to the local monorail station, travel hundreds of miles in an hour or so, then get off for another short bike ride to your destination. What with the shortage of energy-producing resources, and the necessity of decreasing the number of air-fouling machines, who knows, people might have to give up their mad love affair with the automobile and go back to using their pedaling muscles. I'm not going to bet on it, but I'm sure going to use my own pedaling muscles in the meantime.

Getting a bicycle onto most modes of public transportation isn't easy. Sometimes it isn't even allowed. Cyclists have to exert pressure on the transit companies, railroads, airlines, etc., to get better transportation. This means letter-writing, lobbying, buttonholing. Join a strong bike club, like one of the Wheelmen groups, or the American Youth Hostels, and a tough conservation group as well, and they will inform you about how you might best get into the fight for a better set-up. Right now, cycling is very well thought of, and even enjoyed, by people in positions of great power. Mrs. Henry Ford II, for instance, is an avid cyclist. That's a twist. Henry Senior got his start in bikes, you know, but I'd hate to see the product if FoMoCo went back to producing them.

To improve the chances for public transportation, use whatever services are offered for cyclists. If there is a pilot program, go out of your way to use it, so that more significant services will be developed because of the demand. Hopefully the meager services outlined below will expand with the increase in cycling interest.

TRAINS

The railroads allow fold-up bikes, like the Raleigh Twenty, to be taken aboard if they are folded up. For commuting, the fold-up is obviously the best bike—you can take it into the train, the streetcar, the elevator, and even the office, and ride whenever it's convenient.

For longer train trips, such as the one shown in the "Tour Trips" chapter, call the railroad ticket office and make sure you are allowed to carry your bike as excess baggage. If you have a large bike, it can often be put in the baggage car and taken for quite reasonable rates. For example, the 280 mile train trip from San Jose to Santa Barbara, in California, was made by a bike for only $2.14 at the time this book was written. There are holes in the service though. Always call the railroad ticket agent to check out the service before you go down to the station with your bike.

BUSES

The vast majority of metropolitan and suburban bus systems have no way to cope with bicycles. Bicycles are too hard to get into and out of buses. They take up too much room. They poke the other passengers. If you have to commute via bus, you can try to take a fold-up, like the Raleigh Twenty, on board with you, and you may get away with it, especially if the folded-up bike is in a bag that will protect people from the bike's sharp protuberances. But you will run into drivers who don't allow even fold-ups on their buses. Hopefully, the situation will change. But the change will probably come only after cyclists have gotten together and pressured for it. Join a bike club and write letters to the transit companies.

Long-distance bus trips can be made with a fold-up bike like the Raleigh Twenty folded up and put in a sack. In the case of larger, less collapsible bikes, they must be dismantled and put into cartons. The easiest way to do this is to go to a bike shop and ask them for a carton, and at the same time, try to get a look at one of their new bikes as it comes out of the carton, so you can see how to put yours back in. Depending on the size of the carton and the bike, you may have to dismantle more or less. Standard procedure involves taking off the front wheel, the seat, the handlebars and stem, and the pedals. To get the front wheel off, loosen the big nuts or wing-nuts on the axle, or pull out on the quick-release lever if you have one. Remove the handlebars by loosening the bolt whose head sticks up at the back of the stem. Tap that bolt head when it is about two turns loose, and it will disengage the stem. If you have hand brakes, be careful as you jockey around with the handlebars. It's easy to kink the brake cables. To remove the seat, loosen the binderbolt that pinches the frame around the seat post. The pedals unscrew from the cranks, but remember that the left pedal is reverse threaded—unscrew it clockwise, instead of counter-clockwise.

When you get all those things off the bike, work out some way to weave the handlebars in and out of the frame so that the whole business will fit into the carton. This may require loosening the bolt that holds the handlebars in the stem. When you have wrangled the frame, rear wheel, and handlebars into the carton, figure some way to get the front wheel in there. Put the pedals, the seat, and any loose bolts and nuts in a sack and tie them to the frame. Tape and rope the carton closed securely—bus drivers aren't known for their finesse with luggage.

FERRIES

Most ferries that carry cars will carry bicycles, and if there is a fee, bikers usually pay the pedestrian rate. If you are ever in the area, try the Sausalito to San Francisco ferry that's run by the Golden Gate Bridge Company. It's the most luxurious ferry I've seen, and there are, at commuting hours, dozens of friendly cyclists aboard. In Southern California, the Catalina ferries are good, and there is an annual cycle outing that covers the whole island. On the Eastern Seaboard, there's the old stand-by, the Staten Island ferry, but Staten Island has gotten more trafficky recently. In Maine, the Boothbay Harbor ferries to the outlying islands can be fun if the weather is decent. Martha's Vineyard off Massachusetts is nice too, if it isn't too windy. Or try the long ferry out to Nassau from Miami. Sorry, but there aren't any youth hostels on the island.

In the Midwest, Washington Island in northern Lake Michigan is great during the warmer months of the year.

AIRPLANES

The airlines have no standard rules, regulations, or prices for bicycle transportation. You must realize, though, that bicycles are a problem for the airlines. Their baggage is often comprised of many puncturable items, like canvas suitcases, and the people and machines that handle airline luggage are hard on it. This means that if you put a bike through the works, it might come back with someone's underwear festooned all over it, or it might come back in pieces after having been digested by one of the machines. For the safety of the bike and the luggage, box your bike if you want to take it on an airplane. Follow the packing instructions under the Buses section above. One added precaution for plane transportation: Cut a little block, one inch by one inch by about four inches, or the right length so it just fits between the drop-outs of the front fork. Put the block between the drop-outs and hammer a nail into either end to make sure it stays there. That way, the forks can't get mashed together. You might write FRAGILE all over the carton, too, and pray a little, for good measure.

Among the airlines researched, the ones with the best deal were the local or regional commuter airlines. They often make no extra charge for a cartoned bicycle. One international airline, Swissair, charges only a dollar extra for a cartoned bike. Just call your favorite airline when you want to fly with your bike, then get a carton, dismantle the bike, pack it well, and take it as extra luggage. Airplanes are one form of transportation on which the fold-up bike does not do well. Unless the bike is not only folded, but also cartoned well, it will be vulnerable to damage in the luggage compartment and on the airport conveyor belts.

If you plan to fly to Europe and cycle there, for heaven's sake don't take a bike with you. Find the name and address of a good bike maker near where you are going to land (the consulate will supply info like that) and get a new bike there. They are much cheaper over there. You can also rent bikes inexpensively in many parts of Europe, if you don't want to buy a new one.

PRIVATE CAR

If it is impossible or ridiculously inconvenient to use mass transportation to take your bike a long distance in a short time, you are left with having to use the trusty smog maker. If you have a car or truck with a lot of room inside, the simplest and safest way to transport a bike is inside. Even if this means taking off the front wheel and doing some back-seat gymnastics, it should be tried before the bike is carried outside the car where it can be squashed, wind-battered, or stolen. You have a little car? You are perhaps sick and tired of getting grease all over the back seat, and bumping your head on the door frame? OK, you need an alternative.

1978 Ford Model Z

Two fairly inexpensive alternatives are the bumper-type carrier, and the car-top carrier. The first is simpler, but more expensive, and requires a couple of changes to be rendered functional for great amounts of use. The second, the car-top carrier, is cheap, extremely efficient, and able to carry more bikes comfortably. But it takes a little carpentry and scrounging around to get together, and it takes a little finesse to get the bikes on and off, especially if the car is high, and the bikes are heavy.

BUMPER-TYPE CARRIER, INSTALLATION AND USE

A number of different companies now make variations of the original bumper-type carrier or Bike Toter. There is one particularly good, although costly, collapsible one that is not only convenient, but also stronger than the others. You can use it on straight-bumpered cars without making any changes at all. Most of the others require some degree of shoring up, though, if you are going to give them heavy use. First of all, after you have the carrier frame assembled, you must be sure the thing is firmly secured to the bumper. If your bumper is strong, and the hook-bolts supplied with your carrier fit around the bumper well, slip the bolt ends through the lowest holes on the carrier uprights that you can. This will make the carrier as high as possible, keeping the bikes up off the ground. Then tighten up the nuts for the hook-bolts. Hard. If the bumper is weak, it will bend out. In that case, get some big "U" bolts that will fit around your bumper and through the holes in the carrier frame. Put small blocks of wood behind your bumper, get the "U" bolts around the blocks and the bumper, and you can tighten up hard without discombobulating your ½ mile per hour bumper.

People who carry two or three bikes on a bumper-type carrier run into the problem of the carrier frame bending away from the car. To avoid this malady, find some edge on the car body as near as possible to the top of the carrier frame, like the edge of a trunk or hood, or the grating of a ventilator hole, where you can attach a hook on the end of a strong strap, cord, or chain. Run the strap or whatever from the attaching place on the body of the car to the top bar of the bike carrier. Two such support straps, one at each end of the top of the carrier, are better than one.

You will notice that the bumper-type carrier often makes it difficult to open the trunk or (in the case of VW's) hood of your car. One solution which works especially well on VW's is to get a piece of one-inch angle iron and make a longer top bar for your carrier. Drill four holes in the angle iron, two at the ends for the bolts that go into the ends of the carrier uprights,

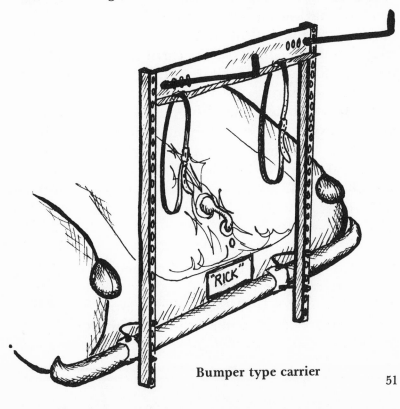

Bumper type carrier

and two holes closer together for the arms that stick out and hold the bikes. Measure carefully before you drill these holes. You want the outer ones far enough apart so that the car trunk or hood will fit between the uprights, and you want the inner two holes close enough together to allow the carrier arms to fit under the top tube of your bike. If you have to do a lot of altering and shoring up to your bumper-type carrier, you might well ask, why did I buy a carrier in the first place? Answer—for its sturdy uprights. But if you can get your own sturdy uprights somewhere, you can build your own carrier from scratch. Just make sure it's tall enough to keep the bikes well up off the ground. (P.S. A *strong* wide VW rack is now made in Sausalito, California. At last!)

To protect the paint of bicycles being carried on a bumper-type carrier, especially on long car trips over bumpy roads, tie rags around the bikes where they are going to knock against each other. Thread any rope that's going to hold a bike to the carrier under the brake cables and housings, so the cable doesn't cut into the bike's paint. To pad the carrier itself permanently, you can take an old bike inner tube, slice out the section with the valve, and wrap the remaining long tube around the parts of the carrier which the bike is going to hit. Tie the ends tightly, or tape them down. The bikes should be tied tightly on the carrier, too, to keep them from swinging and joggling around.

When you are driving a car with a bumper-type carrier and bikes on the back, watch out for sharp dips, or the entrances to steep driveways—the bikes tend to whack the ground. Also, be extra careful as you back into and out of parking places.

CAR-TOP CARRIER, INSTALLATION AND USE

A sturdy car-top bike carrier is relatively cheap to install. Buy a two-bar carrier with fittings that clamp onto the rain gutters of your car (see illustration). That kind is much more stable than the suction cup kind. The carrier should cost somewhere between $10 and $15.

Decide how many bikes you are going to want to carry. If they are placed end to end, as many as six bikes can be taken on a car, but this requires accurate placement of the mounting blocks. Cut two by three inch blocks out of two by four douglas fir, or hardwood for extra strength. File a one inch wide, rounded groove in each of the blocks, as shown. Take five inch sections of old bike inner tube and nail them in the grooves for padding. To find out where you are going to mount the blocks on the bars, line your bikes up, right side up, in the same positions they will assume on top of the car. Then lay the carrier bars upside down across the handlebars and mark the places where each stem (gooseneck) of a bike crosses the carrier bars. You can then pick two mounting blocks, one for each side of the stem mark. You need to leave about

two to three inches between the mounted blocks,
depending on the width of the stem and the width of
the horizontal section of the handlebars. Put the loose
blocks on your handlebars to get the measurement
just right. Then attach the blocks to the carrier bars
with pan-head or round-head wood screws. Often the
carrier bar has convenient holes drilled in it for these
screws, but if it doesn't, you have to drill them, using
a high-speed drill bit if the carrier bar is metal. Make
sure you screw the screws in good and tight, because
the handlebar mounting blocks do the bulk of the job
of holding the bikes in place.

When you have the blocks attached to the carrier
bars, you can put one carrier bar on the car. Make sure
the brackets fit snugly in the rain gutters. Measure the
distance from the handlebars to the backs of the seats
on your bikes, then place the second carrier bar the
right distance from the first. This is a problem if you
plan to carry several bikes of different sizes. As long as
the solid backmost part of each seat rests on the carrier
bar, you'll be all right. Don't set the carrier bar in such
a position that its corner digs into the center portion
of the seat, though. That will warp the seat so that it
won't fit your bottom anymore. With both carrier bars
held firmly in place on the car, test the strength of the
gadget. Can you wiggle either bar back and forth? Do
the brackets slip in the gutters if you try to move them?
Make sure everything
is tight enough so it
will stay put when
you are going
seventy miles
an hour with
your beloved
bike on top.

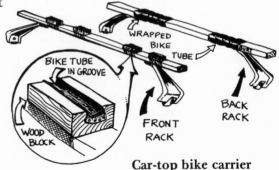

Car-top bike carrier

Lifting bike to top of car

Getting the bike up onto the car-top carrier is tricky. Start by standing the bike, right side up, between you and the car, with the end forward that you are going to have forward on the rack. Reach over the bike with one hand and grab the seat tube from the side of the bike that is *farthest* from you. With the other hand, grab the handlebar that is farthest from you. Lift the bike and flip it in one motion, then set it in place on the rack.

Now, let go of the bike for a second, to pick up that rope you left there on the ground and . . . spend the rest of the day trying to disentangle yourself from the bike that falls on you.

Obviously, you should have some handy means of holding the bike in place once you get it up on the carrier. The simplest method is to have a one foot "Bunjy" or "Sandow" cord—the elastic cord with hooks on the ends—up on the roof of the car, with one end attached to the carrier bar on which the seat of the bike will rest. The attached end of the cord should be on the side of the bike that's away from you, so you can stretch the cord up, around the seat tube of the bike frame, and then down to the end of the carrier bar that's nearest you. Stretch the cord out completely so it will hold the back of the bike steady. Use three or four toe clip straps to hold the handlebars down. These are simple, quick, and as strong as anything else. Besides, for bikes with toe-clips, if you lose one of the straps for holding the bike to the carrier, you can borrow from the bike. Make sure the straps are quite tight. On long trips, check them now and then. To unload the bikes, just reverse the loading procedure.

When driving a car with bikes on top, watch for low overheads, like garages.

TRAILERS

For any bike trip of a group larger than ten, it may prove simpler to rent a trailer to move all the bikes. The best kind of trailer for the purpose is the long flat-bed kind with side rails that are about three feet high. These can be rented from a number of nationwide trailer rental companies. Put the bikes in rows, parallel to the length of the trailer, alternating forward and backward. Try to put all bikes of similar size in each row. When you have a row all in place, stick a two-by-four through all of them, from one side of the trailer to the other, so that you can tie some part of each bike's frame to the board. Depending on the size and gender of the bike, you can tie either the top tube, the seat tube, or the down tube to the two-by-four. Make sure that the board is attached well to the trailer, and you are set to do another row. On a long trailer you can load as many as twenty bikes that way. Don't ever stack bikes on a trailer. They scratch, poke, bend, and despoke each other if you pile them up without respect for their tender parts.

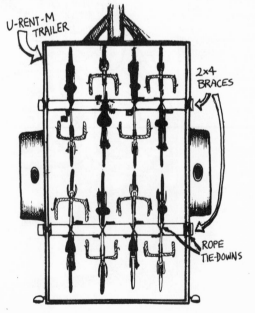

**Top view
of trailer with
bikes**

7 TIPS FOR HAPPY TRIPPING

WHAT TO TAKE WITH YOU WHEN YOU RIDE

Nothing. That's what you should take with you, ideally, on a bike ride. Commuting trips and escape trips, for the most part, are not so long, nor so remote, that you need to take much more than yourself and your bike. As for tools, on a short ride the fun is over if you have a flat or bust a spoke or break a brake cable, whether you bring the tools to repair the damage or not. So fix your bike *before* you go on a ride. Get in the habit of tinkering with your bike, and get a bike that you care enough about to tinker with. You might get a friend, or a good repair manual, to teach you how to keep the bike in good shape, so you can trust it and ride it without having to carry half a tool shop around with you on rides.

Some tools and equipment become a necessity on longer trips. They are listed below in order of importance.

SPARE TIRE. For sew-up people, a spare is necessary even on fairly short rides. For those who use clinchers, on longer rides, take a spare tube and two tire irons, or a patch kit. A spare sew-up or a clincher tube is the quickest answer in case of a flat, but be careful when riding on the spare.

WATER BOTTLE. For all-day trips in hot weather. A plastic or metal bottle held in a bracket on the bike frame. If you sweat a lot, you will need salt tablets, too, so the water you drink won't run right through your body.

BASIC TOOLS. A little (six inch) crescent wrench and a small screwdriver. If there are two riders, the second can carry another crescent, or a pair of pliers. Carry one good, functional pump (like the Silca Impero) too. On long tours, a freewheel remover for ten speeds, and a spoke wrench and some spokes are needed, but should be used by an expert or someone following directions as good as or better than those in my repair manual.

A SMALL FIRST AID KIT (see "Just in Case").

SIMPLE CAMPING EQUIPMENT for the cycle-camping trip. The two basic rules for packing such equipment on a bike are *Keep it light,* and *Balance the load!* That means buy or borrow alpine, super-light sleeping bags, tents, cook stoves, etc. Then put them in a saddle bag or pannier bags on the rear of the bike, and a well-supported handlebar pack at the front of the bike. Good supporting brackets for all the bags can be bought at most serious bike shops. For extra heavy loads, like for extended voyages, special Rene Herse racks are made. Get them from one of the fancy bike shops which specialize in touring equipment. Don't ever carry all your gear in a big back pack. It will make you top-heavy, bottom-weary, and shoulder-sore.

As for air mattresses, suits and ties, cameras and tripods, and the good old kitchen sink, carried in a mini U-haul trailer behind your bike, Bah, humbug!

There's a girl named Dagney who travels by bike, eats in restaurants, and sleeps in hotels. The only luggage she takes is a change of underwear and a nice dress for swanky places. That sounds like a great idea, as long as you don't eat so much that you get sluggish and sloggy. Some of us don't have the bread to travel that way. Try youth hosteling. Join the American Youth Hostels, Inc. (see Addresses) and help them open more hostels. A trip similar to the AYH one is making lots of friends spread out over the map, so you can ride from one to the other, and they can ride to your place for an exchange of hospitality.

HOW MANY SHOULD GO

The standard bicycle is designed to give one person a wonderfully reliable and independent means of transportation. Why not use your bike that way? Get out of the whole social scene when you take a bike trip. Cycling can be an escape to self and to selfless enjoyment of one's natural surroundings. If you like groups, get big ones together for political action, like they did in Los Angeles to publicize the need for bike trails. But then try riding on the trails by yourself some morning.

On short trips, especially beautiful, traffic-free secluded ones like those outlined in the "Short Country Trips" chapter, solo cycling is by far the best. There are exceptions, of course. Group cycling in that atmosphere can be nice, just as going for a stroll with your family or friends can be nice. You can noodle along at the lowest common denominator of speed, and soak up the good vibes of conviviality and fresh air. If, at another extreme, you are doing road training to race, a small group can keep up a stiff pace better than most single cyclists. But that's another type of cycling altogether.

On long trips, it is best to compromise the "solo cyclist" idea because you tend to get lonely riding by yourself. Sometimes, when you are halfway from Nowhere to Podunk, and there's a big hill coming up, you say to yourself, "What the hell am I doing out here? This is the stupidest thing I ever did." At such times, it is good to have a friend along to commiserate with. Just try to pick a fellow cyclist who will go close to the same speed as you on a long trip.

WHEN TO RIDE

If you get up at seven to go to work every day, five days a week, it may be hard for you to get up at six on Saturday or Sunday. But try it. It'll get into your blood after a while. You may have always thought that people are crazy to get up at the crack of dawn on weekends to go shoot guns at birds or whack a little white ball around the countryside. But then you may have noticed also that many good bike tripping areas are beginning to get trafficky on Saturday and Sunday afternoons. In the mornings, these same areas are free of motorized competition and smog.

If you have trouble kicking yourself out of bed, try going outside and taking a deep breath of that fresh, early-morning air. Sometimes that will be enough to make you want to get out on the road. Sometimes grapefruit juice will do the trick. Sometimes you won't feel decent until you've been riding for half an hour.

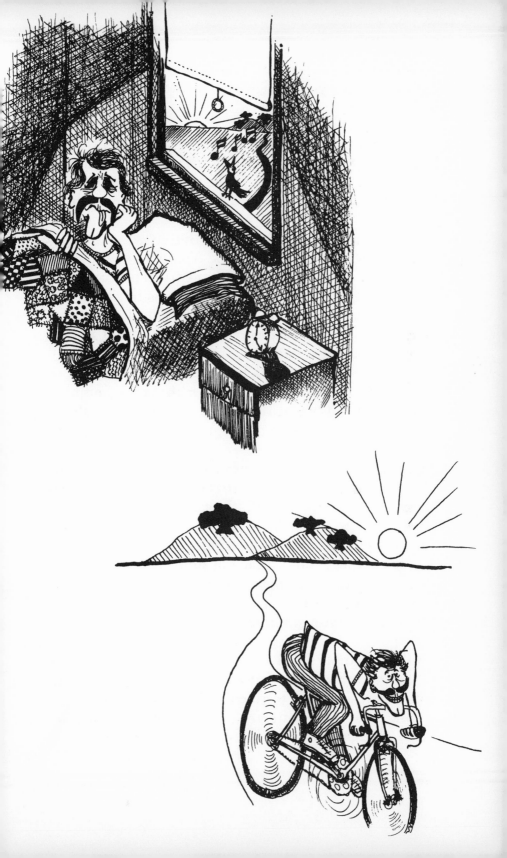

But there will always be a point where you become thankful that you made the effort to get up before the crowds.

On weekdays, in suburbia, there is less traffic between nine and eleven in the morning than there is earlier, during the commuting rush. In the country, the whole morning or even the whole day may be nice. Such ride-anytime rides are rare, though, and getting rarer.

There are times when you definitely should *not* ride. Don't ride when you're drunk. You might think you can do it, but you can't. So don't try. The same is somewhat true of drugs. It's dangerous to ride after putting anything in your body that will slow your reactions, upset your balance, or mess your mind so that your judgment is bad.

Sunday afternoon is a bad time to ride. Sunday drivers tend to miss the forest for the trees, and hit the cyclist for looking at the forest, or barely miss the cyclist and force him to hit a tree, or some awful combination of the three.

Rush hours are bad times to ride. If you commute via bicycle, work out a route that avoids the major auto routes. See "Safety" and "Local Bike Trips" for more hints. Try to take joy rides before, between, or after the rush hours. During the summer, evening sunset rides are nice; many rural and suburban roads become almost deserted during the dinner hours. Just make sure you have a French armband light in case it gets dark before you get home.

WISE RIDING STYLE

There are ways to ride that make cycling a nice trip, and there are ways to ride that make it a pain. First, get a bike that's the right size (see "Which Bike for You") and adjust the seat so that it's level, and at such a height that you are neither folding your legs up too much nor stretching them beyond their normal reach and slopping your fanny back and forth. If, at the bottom of a pedal stroke, you can stretch your leg out straight and rest your foot flat on the pedal, the seat is about right. Keep the bars down, so you bend forward to them, distributing your weight evenly.

On short rides, if the bike fits you, you won't have to use much technique to get along well. Just shift the gears down before you get to any uphill grades, so when you have to start pushing hard on the pedals, you are already in the right gear. Test hand brakes lightly before you actually have to use them on a long downhill, especially if they are wet. As for the care of your own body, if your circulatory system isn't up to par, take it easy, even on short rides. Don't be ashamed to get off and walk up a hill, or even stop altogether if you can feel your pulse throbbing at the temples.

On longer rides, wisdom can play a considerable role in how long you last. Tests have shown that to move a given bike over a given course in a given period of time, a well-trained racing cyclist expends about fifty percent of the energy that a novice uses. It's wise to take a great number of short rides before you try a long ride. The better your feet are trained to make those efficient little circles, the better you'll do. Also, try to get so you lift one foot as you push the other down, so you're not pushing against the dead weight of the foot on the rising pedal.

You'll do best if you adjust your seat and handlebar positions very carefully too; move the seat farther forward and higher if you like pedaling at high rpm and using your toes to push a lot. Move the seat back and down for a slower, more flat-footed pace. Adjust the handlebar stem or even change it for a different extension, to place the bars so you can comfortably use several hand positions, including gripping the brake lever posts.

Set a pace on a long ride and stick to it. Find a good pedaling speed, preferably of more than 75 rpm (that may seem fairly brisk at first, for the average rider) and keep close to that pace, uphill or down. Use the lower range of gears on the uphills, and pedal on the gentle downhill stretches even though it doesn't speed you up much. Don't stop often, or for long rest periods. Eat quick meals or just snacks, and get right back on the bike in less than ten minutes, if possible. This may seem pushy, but it will keep you fresh for much longer than the ride-and-loaf approach. The idea is to keep your muscles in tone. Of course, if they aren't in tone to begin with, a long ride is going to be grueling any way you cut it. But if you are in fair shape, and then set and stick to a pace within your limits, you'll cover more happy miles and less miserable ones. Veloce, the great French bike freak of old, could ride for 48 or 72 hours at a stretch like that.

A brisk, steady pace does things for your morale as well as your muscle tone. If you twiddle up the steep hills in a good low gear, at high rpm, they just seem easier than if you slog up them in a higher gear. Don't flail along needlessly at high rpm, though. Choppy riding, with your body and the whole bike wobbling all over, wastes huge amounts of energy. Concentrate on a smooth stride, your legs and feet making quick, agile circles, but your upper body and the bike moving forward in a perfectly straight line. If you think you are good at making perfect, agile circles with your feet, you can try ankling, the business of tipping your foot back at the top of each stroke, and forward at the bottom of a stroke, to make for a longer power arc. But ankling makes it that much harder for your feet to do smooth, perfect circles without muscles working against each other. Even great racers only use ankling at lower rpm. Look at photos of racers—rarely are they ankling. You're better off spending your time learning to do quick, smooth pedaling. Ankling will come by itself after many years of riding.

While on any long-distance ride, take care of your bodily needs before they become imminent. Drink sparingly before you are thirsty, eat sparingly before you are hungry, and make pit stops for the john before you get uncomfortable. Those things are so simple to say, and yet you'll tend to stretch yourself, trying to ride on just to the next town. Don't.

Take care of gear changes before they become urgent too. As in short distance riding, shift down before you get to a grade, so you are finished shifting before you put heavy pressure on the pedals. Also, it is wise to avoid using the two extreme gear combinations on a ten speed—that of the little front sprocket and little back sprocket, and that of the big front sprocket and the biggest back sprocket. These two extremities overtax the derailleur system and the chain. The gear attained in each case can always be matched by a different combination anyway. Surprise! Your ten speed is really an eight speed.

There are other wise ways of riding that can preserve your bike. Bikes have their weak points. Two of these weak points that must be respected are the tires and the rims.

For longer tire life, watch for glass or nails that might puncture your tires. You may well ask, "How am I supposed to see every little sliver of glass?" You don't have to see every little sliver. It's rare that one sliver of glass will be sitting on the road by itself. Just watch out for patches of glass that mark the spot where there was an accident, or where some damn litterbug threw a bottle. In any intersection, you will notice that

there are triangular patches of gravel and litter. Avoid these. They often harbor hidden glass and tacks. If you have sew-up tires, you may want to use those little wire tire-savers that are attached to the brake mounting bolts and graze along the surface of the tire. There is a great deal of debate as to their effectiveness, but they are worth a try, at any rate. Some racers who use gloves whisk off their tires with a gloved hand every once in a while, instead of using a tire-saver. If you think it's worth the trouble, try it. Be philosophical, though, about that occasional flat. Flats are inevitable, like colds, or the blues.

Rims are delicate. To preserve them, make sure the tires always have enough air pressure in them (see "The Safe Bike"). This will protect the rim when you go over a sharp bump or a chuckhole. Try to avoid extra-bad bumps and deep chuckholes, as well as such obvious rim-wreckers as curbs and slatted storm drains.

To save both tires and rims, as well as avoid a lot of skinned elbows and knees, get into the habit of using proper braking technique. Braking on a bike is quite different from braking in a car. In a car, you see some trouble coming up, and you put your foot down. On a bike with handbrakes, you can't just grab the hand levers and expect to stop without spinning out, falling down, or flipping end over end. Braking on any two-wheeled vehicle takes finesse. Ask motorcycle road-racers. They'll tell you that braking is half the battle.

Make sure you know which handle is attached to which brake on your bike, for a start. If you are riding on smooth pavement, and you realize you have to come to a stop, apply both brakes evenly, then increase the pressure on the *front* brake more than the pressure on the rear brake. The *front* brake should do the bulk of the work in a normal stop. It spooks you to use the front brake? Afraid you're going to fly over the handlebars? Don't be. You won't unless you slam on the front brake without using the rear one at all. The point of using the front brake is that as you slow down, your weight shifts forward, giving the front wheel better traction than the rear wheel. If you hit the rear brake without touching the front one, you'll skid. And in spite of an idiotic law in some states which says that bikes should have a brake "which will enable the operator to make one braked wheel skid on dry, level, clean pavement," the last thing you want to do when you put on your brakes is skid. Skids mean loss of control as well as ruined tires. When the rear wheel skids, even

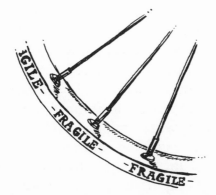

if you're going straight, the bike will tend to slop to one side and lie down, dumping you on the ground.

Braking in curves, especially on gravel-strewn curves, is a lot trickier than on straight and level pavement. In general, the idea is to brake before you have to. If you see a sharp curve coming up, brake early so you won't be caught halfway through the curve going too fast with nothing but skittery gravel ahead. As you go into a curve, you should be letting off the brakes. Let off the front one first, because the front wheel tends to "wash out" or slip from under you if it hits gravel as you lean through a curve. The rear wheel can do a very slight amount of braking in the curve, but the bulk of the work must be done by the front brake before you get into the curve.

For the same reason that you shouldn't brake in a curve, don't shift gears in a curve. And if you are going fast enough to have to lean through the curve, don't pedal, or you might hit the ground with a pedal and do a sudden cartwheel.

JUST IN CASE

Let's hope you never have an accident or any injuries while cycling. But if you do, you should be prepared to perform what first aid you can.

The most frequent cycling injuries are abrasions—skinned elbows, knees, etc. Wash the area of the injury well with soap, or soak it if you can. If you're on a long ride, stop at a gas station and wash the abrasion. If you are skinned under your clothes, like on a hip, try to get a non-sticking bandaid to put over the abrasion so it won't be irritated as you ride.

For any accident which might have caused broken limbs, spine injuries, or head injuries, DON'T MOVE! Get professional help. If you are by yourself, wait till someone comes along, flag him down, and tell him to

Back too hard

BAD BREAKING TECHNIQUE

Front too hard

get help. A broken limb or skull, if improperly handled, can cause fatal internal injury. If there is a serious injury in any group of cyclists, one rider should find out as much as he can about the injury, then ride to the nearest house and phone for an ambulance, doctor, or the fire department. In many rural areas, the fire departments are the best-trained people to call for first aid and transportation to a hospital.

For any accident which causes spurting blood flow from an open wound, direct pressure can be applied, but be very careful if there is any chance of a broken bone in the area of the bleeding.

For heat exhaustion, a frighteningly common summer cycling problem, the symptoms are headache, dizziness, and some confusion. Later there may be nausea and weakness. The person will be pale and sweating a lot, but his skin will be cool to the touch. For relief, lay the person in the shade, but keep him warm. Have someone rub his limbs to keep the blood flowing. Give him tiny sips of water, and small amounts of salt until he feels better. If heat exhaustion turns to heatstroke, i.e., if a person who is pale, sweaty and cold suddenly turns hot, dry, and bright red, then the situation is very bad. Send for a doctor immediately, and cool the person down as fast as possible. Strip him and put him in water or pour water over him. If you can keep him cool by pouring water over him and transport him to a hospital at the same time, do so, but don't put him in a hot car to take him anywhere. His cooling system is kaput, and you MUST keep him cool until a doctor can see him.

For the afflictions of cold weather cycling—numb toes, fingers and ears—wear a good knit cap that fits tightly, and woolen mittens with separations for your fingers and leather patches on the palms. For sub-freezing weather, use fur-lined ski gloves, and thermal stockings, or even those battery-powered electric socks.

For boils or painful pimples in the crotch, give up riding for a few days, if you can. Remind yourself to wash there carefully, and change to fresh underpants often when you cycle a lot. For the men, if you wear jockey shorts, you may notice that the seams of the shorts, where they join, form two painful lumps that push into you as you ride. To avoid the problem, wear boxer shorts, or, if you aren't offended, ladies' cotton underpants with a panel in the crotch and at least two inch long legs. Penney's has them. Sweat pants are good too, because they have the same panel design. Best of course are cycling tights, the funny-looking Peter Pan pants. But they cost a lot.

For beginner's backache or aching wrists, try to build up slowly to riding long distances, and make sure your bike frame, seat, and stem extension are the right size for you. Getting the right combination is hard, especially if your body has odd proportions. Ask a bike dealer for help in getting things right, or see the appropriate sections of a repair manual.

For aching bottom, persevere! If you have a new leather seat, it will take a while for you and the leather to get worn in to each other. On sit-down type bikes, like most three speeds, your seat is going to ache and burn on a long haul, no matter how well you are acquainted with the bike. So stick to shorter rides if you have a bike that by its nature makes your seat hurt.

8 GETTING ON WITH THE ELEMENTS

Cyclists are vulnerable to changes in the weather. Do your riding for enjoyment when the weather is as decent as possible.

If you live in Texas, try riding right around dawn during the summer. The coolest time of the day is an hour or so before sunrise. If you live in Minnesota, most of the year it will be too cold to ride at any but the warmest time of day, some time between one and three in the afternoon, depending on local wind conditions.

Riding in snowy or icy conditions gives very few people enjoyment. For you exceptions, see "Bike Trips for the Fanatic Fringe." If you commute in winter weather, the best way to handle icy pavement is to ride very slowly and try to keep to roads that have been salted or sand-strewn. Be ready at all times to head off into a snow bank to avoid skidding cars. When going down a hill, no matter how slight the grade, be ready at all times to head for a soft landing place if you should lose control or go into a skid. To avoid skids as much as possible, go easy on the brakes and accelerate slowly. Three wheelers are a lot easier than two wheelers in the snow, if you don't mind all the extra weight. For some hints on cold weather clothing, see "Just in Case."

Rain is a bummer. If it is warm rain, you're best off wearing as little as possible, and changing when you get where you're going. If it is cold and rainy, don't ride unless you have to. Wear a long form-fitting raincoat— not a poncho, which has loose corners to catch in the wheels. Wear a hat too, with a long brim behind, like a Sou'wester. Ride slowly, so the wheels don't kick up water and spray you end to end, front and back. Avoid any muddy puddles. They are often deeper than they look. Stay on paved roads, and do things like chain oiling and hub overhauls much more often than you do in dry weather. After any wet run, go over the bike with a soft cloth and dry it off to prevent rust. Don't leave the bike in the rain, no matter how new or old or fancy or plain it is. How would you like to be left out in the rain, all naked, with your joints open to the weather? You wouldn't like it any better if you were old and arthritic, either.

Wind, the invisible element, is disregarded by most travelers. But to the cyclist, wind is of the utmost importance. A stiff tailwind can increase speed by 50 percent. A strong headwind can reduce the cyclist to a blithering, dead-tired mess. When planning a bike trip of any distance, try to psyche out the wind beforehand. This isn't easy. But you can at least learn what the prevailing winds are in a given area, and then learn some of the basic things about local thermal and terrain-controlled winds, so that you can make educated guesses as to which way the winds are going to blow, before you get out and tangle with them.

First, remember the general rule that winds blow least early in the morning, and most in the early part of the afternoon. If you are making a loop ride, in other words, ride against the wind in the morning, and let the increasing prevailing wind blow you back towards home in the afternoon.

To learn what the prevailing winds are in your area for any given time of year, look at the appropriate map of the U.S. on these pages, check the arrow next to the city nearest you for the prevailing wind direction, then look at the little sunburst around the city to see how often the wind actually blows in the prevailing direction. The sunburst rays have nothing to do with the sun. The rays point out the wind directions. The number in the middle of the sunburst tells you what percentage of the time during the month there is no appreciable wind at all. The length of each little ray of the sunburst tells you how often the wind blows *from* the direction in which the ray points.

Some examples will make things clearer. Let's pretend you live in Brownsville, Texas, and you want to go on a ride in July. Turn to the July map of the U.S. and find Brownsville, the southernmost town in the country. Look at that prevailing wind arrow. You are obviously not going to want to ride twenty miles or so out of town to the northwest, then turn around and have to struggle against the wind all the way home. Brownsville doesn't lend itself to long rides to the east, because of the water there, but you might try riding down into Mexico a ways, then letting the wind blow you back up to town. If you live in Brownsville, you won't be able to count on having any completely calm days during July, because the little number in the middle of the sunburst shows that it is dead calm only two percent of the time. And that might well be at night. So for short, twenty-mile or less country escape trips around Brownsville, or towns like it with very lopsided sunbursts, leave early in the day and ride first *towards* the wind, in the directions that the long sunburst rays point. Then you can sail home with the wind.

If you are planning a long trip north from Brownsville in July, like up to Corpus Christi or even up to Austin, you can tell that the wind will be behind you all the way. The prevailing wind arrows for Austin, Galveston, and Corpus Christi all point to the north, and there are virtually no sunburst rays pointing to the north from any of those cities.

For a somewhat more difficult example, look at the U.S. wind map for April, and pretend you live in Boston. The prevailing wind is neither strong nor constant in its direction. For this sort of wind condition, it is

OCTOBER

best to limit country escape trips to short rides, early in the day, and in areas where there are alternate routes, so you can shorten any ride if it gets unpleasantly windy. One way to avoid most of the wind problems around places like Boston is to ride into the prevailing wind and uphill on your way out on any trip, then you can come back downhill without much trouble even if the wind does turn and blow against you. For longer trips, try to break them up into short, 40 mile segments or less, and ride in the morning. Also, try riding in small groups, so each of you can take a turn at the lead, while the others "sit in" right behind, taking advantage of the leader's draft.

There are some areas where the winds blow in opposing directions. Take Phoenix, for instance, on the July map. The prevailing wind is not only weak—it isn't the main wind. The most common winds, according to the sunburst rays, are one which blows from the east (this wind happens to blow during the night and early morning), and one which blows from the west in the afternoon, especially on those hot summer days. Now, there's no way you can tell *when* the winds blow from the different directions by looking at the U.S. wind maps, but in cases like Phoenix, the surrounding terrain gives you a tip-off. Phoenix is in a valley, surrounded by mountains. On warm days, the slopes of the mountains and steep upper valleys heat up first, before the valley floor. Air rises off the mountains, and by afternoon, wind is being sucked up from the valley to fill the gap. Breezes like this, known as "valley breezes," are common in many hilly parts of the country on warm afternoons. At night, the mountains cool quickly, and the valleys stay warm, so air rises off the lower valleys and cold mountain air rushes down the slopes to fill the gap. These "mountain breezes" or katabalic or drainage breezes appear during the nights and early mornings following hot days in many mountainous parts of the country. They can make early morning riding, especially pre-dawn riding up a valley, cold and miserable, even when the daytime temperatures in the same area are high. If you live in an area that has local wind conditions like those in Phoenix, during the warmest parts of the year, you may want to ride from eight to twelve in the morning, instead of earlier. Sometimes there might be a calm period just before sunset for riding. Otherwise, try to do your uphill riding in the afternoon, and your downhill trips during the early morning, to keep the wind at your back.

Another example of winds that blow diurnally in opposite directions can be found in coast towns. Turn to the U.S. wind map for January, and look at Los Angeles. There are winds blowing from the west and the east, according to the sunburst rays. The west winds blow in the afternoons, and the east winds blow in the night and early morning. These are the familiar land and sea breezes. During the day, the land heats up faster than the sea, air rises over the land, and the wind blows in from the sea to fill the gap. These on-shore winds blow strongest between noon and three or so in the afternoon. The off-shores blow as the land cools, between sunset and eight or nine in the evening. So if you want to avoid the breezes, ride in the morning, or just before sunset. Remember, too, that these coastal breezes can appear even when the prevailing winds indicated on the map are different. In Charleston, for instance, on the July U.S. wind map, the prevailing winds are from the south. But on-shore and off-shore breezes can be expected as well.

The fact is, the wind is the result of an infinitely complex interplay of different factors, only a few of which are described here. But if you learn the basics, and how to combine your knowledge of the prevailing

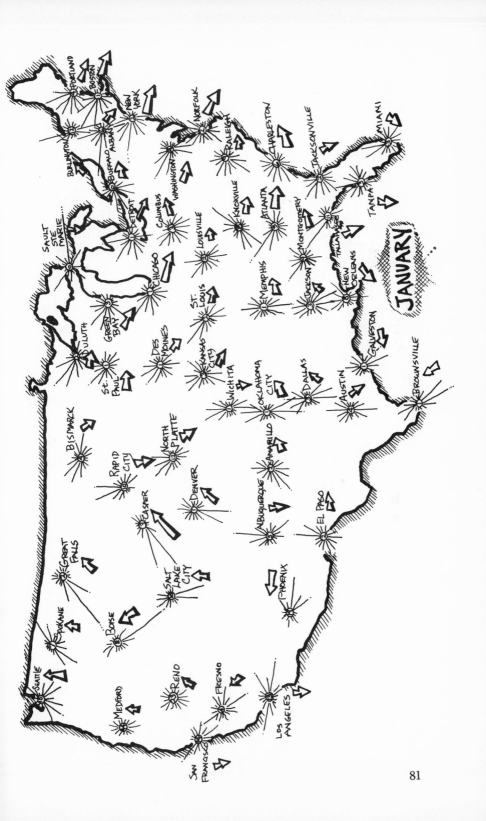

JANUARY

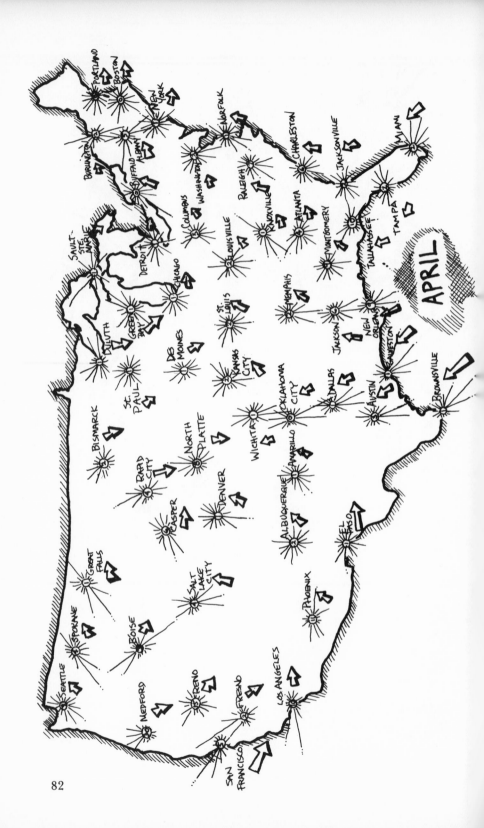

APRIL

wind with a familiarity of your local terrain, geology, and daily heat changes, you can make fairly educated guesses as to which direction the wind is going to arrive from, and plan your bike trips to keep it coming from behind you.

One other way of keeping one step in front of the wind is to phone ahead. If you are going to ride a long distance, or drive some distance out of a town and then do a lot of riding, call a friend who lives in the area, or call the local police or fire department, or coast guard if you're going to be near the coast.

With forethought, you can not only avoid the most unpleasant elemental problems, but actually use some of them to your advantage.

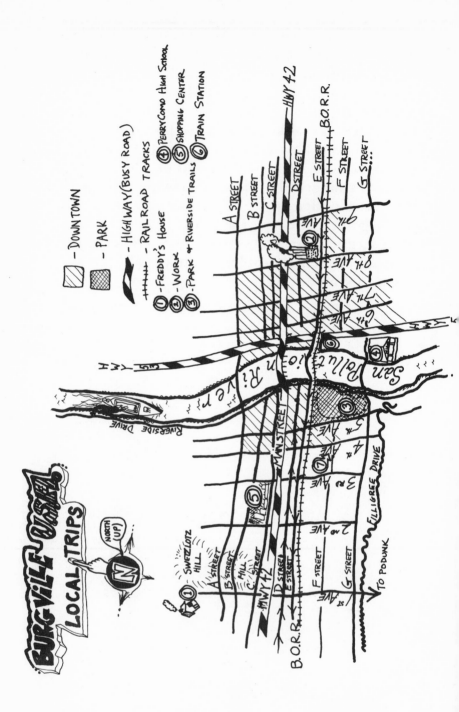

BURGVILE USA LOCAL TRIPS

LEGEND

☐ — DOWNTOWN
▨ — PARK
▨ — HIGHWAY (BUSY ROAD)
┼┼┼┼ — RAILROAD TRACKS
‧‧‧‧ — FREDDY'S HOUSE
① — FREDDY'S HOUSE
② — WORK
③ — PARK & RIVERSIDE TRAILS
④ — PERRY COMO HIGH SCHOOL
⑤ — SHOPPING CENTER
⑥ — TRAIN STATION

NORTH (UP)

N

84

You can do an amazing amount of your short-distance traveling on a bike, instead of in a smogmobile. If you live in a small town, or a suburb, or even in a quieter neighborhood of a big city, you can learn to take routes that mix good transportation and ecology vibes with enjoyment and escape from the humdrum. Do at least part of your daily commuting and/or shopping via bicycle, and it will break up the routine, like recess used to when you were a kid.

The accompanying map of Burgville, U.S.A. is not a map of a real place. But it has many attributes of typical towns and suburb communities all over the country. If you read this section carefully and follow the indicated trips on the map, you can apply the abstract principles of local route-finding to your own community. For city dwellers, the ideas are the same, but you just have to be ready to deal with more congestion and things like one-way streets with high-speed through traffic, which should be avoided if possible. The whole idea is to seek out the routes that will keep you away from the high-speed or clotted auto traffic and take you through the "green belts" or quiet areas that can make the trip nice.

Let's take, as an example, Freddy Sprocketooth, who lives in that little house (1) on First Avenue just above A Street, in Burgville. Freddy Sprocketooth is a lucky cyclist. He lives in a nice town, with only one difficult hill to climb, and ideal weather for cycling most of the year.

Freddy is also smart about the routes he picks to get to and from his job, his shopping, and his dates with the voluptuous Beula Ashta. If you follow his example, you might find some pleasant cycling near you, though you'll probably also find that you don't

live in as convenient a town as Burgville. You and
your surroundings are real, after all, and the trips in
this book are made up. Hallucinated, and therefore
unlike any down-to-earth trips on bicycles. Just learn
from the way surreal Freddy gets around, and do
your own trips accordingly.

Freddy works in a big factory (2) that is all the way
across town from where he lives, at Eighth Avenue and
D Street. To get to work, Freddy could hop on his
trusty old three speed, go down First Avenue, turn left
on Highway 42, or Main Street as it is known in Burgville, then ride across the river to Eighth Avenue, where
he would turn right to get to the factory. That would
be the logical route a car would take. But Freddy wants
to stay off the car routes. So he finds ways to go that
parallel the traffic routes. The simplest one goes from
Freddy's house on First Avenue to A Street, then goes
left on A Street, over the hill and across the river on
the A Street bridge, to Eighth Avenue, where Freddy
turns right and rides down to his job. That route is
fairly direct, and good if Fred is feeling up to pumping
his trusty but heavy three speed over Swetzlotz Hill.
Sometimes he wakes up feeling dragged out, though.
He has an alternative route for such mornings. He goes
down First Avenue, across Main Street and the railroad
tracks, all the way to G Street. He turns left on G
Street, and rides to the city park. He cuts through the
park, goes over the foot bridge and through Perry Como
High School. Then he follows G Street again to Eighth
Avenue, where he turns left and goes up to the factory.
This route is pleasant and easy, but it takes a little
longer. If Freddy is late for work, he has learned that
the quickest route is down to A Street, then left and
over the hill to the shopping center (5). He cuts diagonally across the parking lots (which are empty at that
hour of the morning), takes the Main Street bridge over

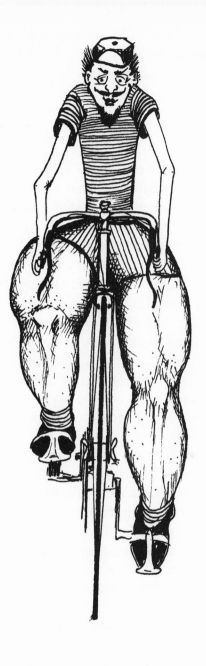

Freddy Sprocketooth

the river, and follows Main to Eighth Avenue, where he turns right to get to the factory. This way is neither pleasant nor particularly safe, so Freddy uses it only when he is late for work.

For the trip home, Freddy rarely feels like pumping up over Swetzlotz Hill. He usually feels like taking a quiet route, so he can calm his frazzled nerves, and maybe even have a little self-to-self talk in peace, hashing out that conversation he had with the boss, saying what he really felt like saying at the time, while noodling along a quiet lane towards home. For this sort of route, Freddy goes down Eighth Avenue from the factory to G Street, then turns right on G and goes to Perry Como High. He crosses through the empty schoolgrounds, over the foot bridge, and then follows the park and riverside trails down to Filligree Drive, which winds through the ritzy residential section of Burgville. When Fred has meandered along the shady, quiet length of Filligree Drive, he comes out on First Avenue, and turns right to ride up to his home, probably feeling a lot more refreshed than if he had taken a double martini at the local dive.

This is not to say that the riverside trails and the winding ritzy lanes of your area are bound to be nice and to your taste. Sometimes the San Polluto Rivers stink, and sometimes the rich neighborhoods are gaudy and treeless. But there is always a way to go home from work that takes you through some quieter, more pleasant area. Just take a little extra time on the way home, and find a park to ride through, or a quiet older neighborhood.

If Freddy is in a rush to get home, he can always take E Street, which is one way, all the way from the factory to First Avenue, then turn right and ride up to his home. But E Street is busy during the rush hour, and because it is a one-way street with synchronized

Buela Ashta

signals, the traffic is not only heavy, but fast-moving. So Freddy usually opts for G Street and the footbridge from Como High to the city park.

Fred does most of his light shopping at the shopping center that runs along Main Street between Second and Fourth Avenue. He can get to the shopping center via A Street, pumping up over Swetzlotz Hill and coasting down to the back entrance of the shopping center parking lots, thus avoiding traffic. But when his bike basket is full of groceries or clothes or Transvaal daisies or whatever, his trusty three speed is that much heavier, and he doesn't want to have to struggle back over the hill. Neither does he want to have to negotiate a lot of traffic, as he would if he took Main Street. So he takes C Street, a short, quiet back street, from the corner of the shopping center back to First Avenue, then rides up to his home on First.

Sometimes Freddy goes to visit Beula Ashta in the evening. He never forgets to take the necessary paraphernalia for such occasions, of course. For night trips he has a French armband light. He gets to Beula's house (7) at F Street and Fourth Avenue by going over the hill on A Street to Fourth, then down through town on Fourth to Beula's. On the way home he often isn't up to Swetzlotz. Also, he avoids downtown and the lonely riverside trails, because he has learned that people think gags like stick-stuck-in-the-spokes are funny downtown, or out in the dark on Saturday night, though such gags are unthinkable at any other time and place. So Freddy takes G Street and First Avenue home, riding slowly, with his little red light turned on and bobbing up and down all the way.

Freddy finds a few minutes whenever he can to take a short pleasure trip on his bike. He has a fancy bike that he uses for all local pleasure bike trips, longer country escape trips, and tours. It is much lighter and

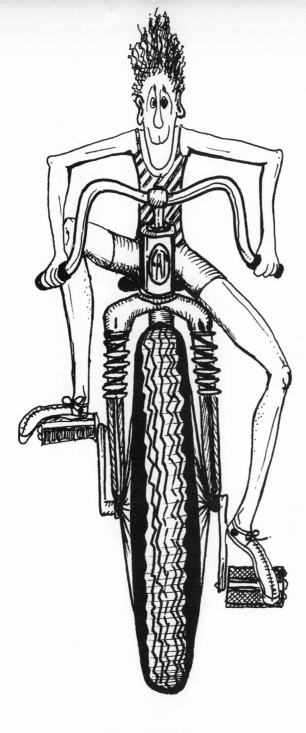

Skinny Shawinny

Patty Fattire

more fun to ride than his commuting bike, but he never uses it for shopping and riding to work because he can't leave it parked anywhere without worrying about it being ripped off. For a short pleasure ride from Freddy's house, he can take the good bike down First Avenue to Filligree Drive, then through the tree-lined length of Filligree to the river. At the river he can turn right and follow the riverside trails, or turn left and take a loop or two through the park. To finish the mini-tour, Freddy follows Riverside Drive along the river through town and up to A Street. Riding over Swetzlotz Hill on A Street gives him a nice work-out to finish off the ride. He gets home feeling exercised, and better able to do whatever it was that prevented him from taking a longer country escape trip. Freddy often takes this same route, or one similar to it, if he goes cycling on a Saturday morning with Beula, and another slower riding couple, Skinny Shawinny and his gal, Patty Fattire. The group takes the ride at a leisurely, strolling pace, and a fine time is had by all.

Freddy's work often requires that he take the train to Megatonopolis, a city of some size, 50 miles away from Burgville. Fred rides his around-town bike to the station via First Avenue, G Street, the footbridge, Como High, and Highway 53. When he comes back to Burgville from the city, he usually wants some exercise in the fresher Burgville air, so he rides one block east from the train station to Sixth Avenue. He turns left on Sixth and rides up to A Street, then rides over Swetzlotz Hill on A Street to First Avenue and home.

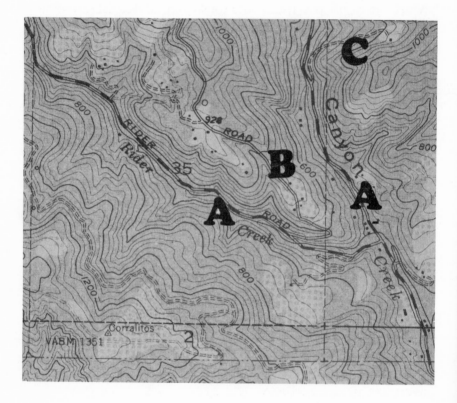

"Topo" Map

A = Good close-to-level roads
B = Steep lesser road
C = Baaad road

Freddy needs to escape for a while now and then.
We all do. To escape, some of us immerse ourselves in
a hobby, like cloud-watching. Some of us drink a little
too much. Some of us blow dope. Some of us medi-
tate. Whatever. Fred trips out on his bike, his good
bike, which is light and responsive and definitely a
good trip to ride. Such a good trip is it to ride, in fact,
that he never feels hung-over afterwards, or groggy or
headachey or left with a suspicion that it was all a
hoax. He comes back from his trip feeling tired, the
great kind of tired you can feel only after doing physical work that was so much fun you didn't know you
were working at all.

Freddy takes whatever Short Country Escape route
he feels up to. He is lucky, in that he lives in a town
with a lot of various escape routes around it. But even
if he lived in Megatonopolis, he could always find good
bike tripping areas by following some simple rules.

If you live in a city or suburb, assume you live at or
near the hub of a wheel, the spokes of which are the
main highways out to other cities. To get to good bike
tripping areas, drive out a spoke-highway, then find
quiet lesser roads either between the spokes or parallel
to them. Good maps make the job of finding between-
the-spokes rides easier. AAA maps are better than most.
They are available to members of the club. Join, or find
a friend who is a member. U.S. Geological Survey topographical maps are an alternative. They give you an
accurate picture of how steep roads are by the use of
elevation or contour rings. Sometimes they are dated,
though, listing non-existent roads, or failing to show
newly built freeways. But they're often the best maps
available to the cyclist. To get "topo" maps, see your
regional office of the U.S. Geological Survey, or send

orders, with 50 cents for each map, to either of the national distribution offices (see Addresses). Some hiking, camping, and skiing stores have topo maps, but these maps are often only of wilderness areas.

Whatever map you get, look on it for the lesser roads that aren't:

  a) thick, straight lines to a recreation area or town
  b) too thin and squiggly, which means poorly made and steep
  c) running along mountain ridges; valley roads, ones that follow streams or rivers, are usually closer to level.

With a little experience, you'll be able to pick out the decent rides on a map without even having seen the area before.

On the imaginary map, Burgville is on one of the spokes (Highway 42) that lead out of Megatonopolis. Therefore, if Freddy looks either north or south of Burgville for quiet, lesser roads, he is bound to find some good bike trips. Indeed, Freddy has found a whole bag of good routes.

If he doesn't feel like doing a whole lot of work for his bike trip, as is sometimes the case on a morning after a rough night before, Freddy rides through the quiet farmland that is south and west of Burgville. Starting in town, he goes south to Podunk. He can then turn left on Podunk Road and ride to the river, turn left again, and ride along the river back to town. A longer ride in the same vein can be taken to Podunk Road, then right to Simms Road. At Simms Road, Freddy turns left, rides south under the freeway, and continues to Kutt Road. He makes a left on Kutt, rides to the river, then returns on the River Road to town. These roads offer some nice scenery, little traffic, and easy pedaling, as there are no hills. The only problem Freddy sometimes encounters is the wind. Around noon, on warm days, the wind blows north, off Lake Wuzblue and across the flat farmland. Late in the afternoon of a warm day, as the air cools, the wind blows south, back towards the lake. So Freddy tries to ride towards the lake before the wind comes up, and towards home before the wind switches directions in the late afternoon (for the reasons behind this common wind phenomenon, see "Getting on with the Elements"). Sometimes Fred and one or two friends take an even longer farmland trip, starting early and riding west from Burgville on Highway 42 to Wuzblue Heights, and returning via Podunk Road, Simms Road, Kutt Road, and the River Road. This ride almost always involves some wind-bucking, but with a group of riders it isn't so rough. Each can take a turn at riding first, while the others "sit in" right behind the leader, taking advantage of the windbreak.

On some mornings, when the air is fresh and Freddy is fresh from a good night's sleep, he feels like a stiffer challenge than the farmland rides offer. He takes to the hills. For a fairly short but invigorating ride, Freddy can start in Burgville and ride over the steep foothills on Bart Road (note the squiggly section—that's where it's the steepest). At the Old Cold Rapids Highway, Freddy turns left, and rides along a valley floor (that's where the road is relatively straight) then turns right on the Last Chance Road, a narrow gravel road that goes over a range of the Guano Mountains and then winds down to the park that spreads along the west fork of the San Polluto River. Freddy crosses the shallow river at a ford, turns right after crossing, and follows a park road along the east bank to where the Old Cold Rapids Highway bridges the west fork of the river. At that point he recrosses the river, and follows the Old Cold Rapids Highway back to Bart Road, on which he turns left and pumps over the hills to Burg-

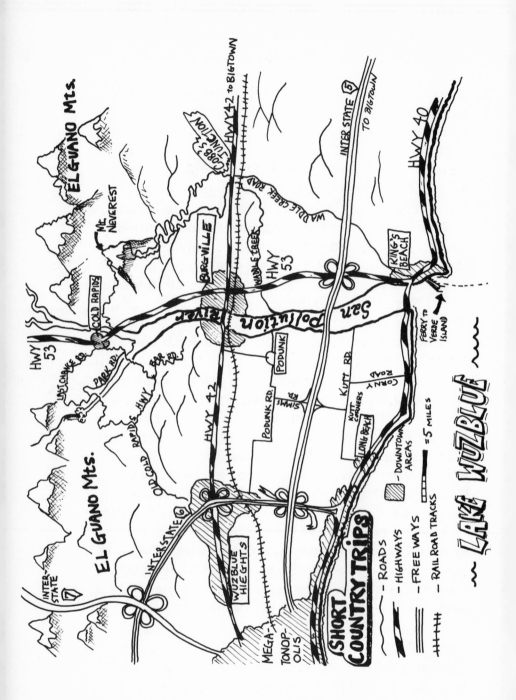

~ LAKE WUZBLUE ~

SHORT COUNTRY TRIPS

- ROADS
- HIGHWAYS
- FREE WAYS
- RAIL ROAD TRACKS

DOWNTOWN AREAS

= 5 MILES

INTER-STATE 7

EL GUANO Mts.

INTERSTATE 7

MEGA-TONOPOLIS

WUZBLUE HIEGHTS

HWY 42

OLD COLD RAPIDS HWY

PARK RD.

LAST CHANCE RD.

HWY 53

COLD RAPIDS

Mt. NEVEREST

EL GUANO Mts.

BOB RD.

San Pollution River

BURGVILLE

WADDLE CREEK

HWY 53

COBB'S JUNCTION

HWY 42 to BIGTOWN

WADDLE CREEK ROAD

PODUNK

PODUNK RD.

SIMMS RD.

KUTT CORNERS

KUTT RD.

CORNY ROAD

LONG BEACH

INTER STATE 5

TO BIGTOWN

KING'S BEACH

FERRY TO VERDE ISLAND

HWY 40

98

ville, tired, perspiring even if it's cold, and relaxed.

If Freddy gets up some morning bursting with energy, or so mad at something that he has to let off steam, he can start early, before the morning traffic, and ride up Highway 53 to Cold Rapids, then take the tortuous Waddell Creek Road over Mt. Neverest (any squiggly road to a mountain top, or over a high ridge, is bound to be a nasty one) and back down a hair-raising, windy grade to Cobb's Junction. At Cobb's Junction Freddy can call it a day, and take the short but trafficky ride via Highway 42 back into Burgville.

If he still has steam to burn, Freddy can continue on the Waddell Creek Road all the way down to King's Beach. At King's Beach, he can cross the San Polluto River, then ride back up the River Road to Burgville, hopefully with an afternoon breeze helping him along. The whole ride is about 60 miles long, and about half of it is in the mountains. When Freddy makes it home, he will have that terrific spent feeling that is such a nice release of pent-up steam or oats.

Sometimes Freddy has lots of steam and/or calories to burn, but little time to go pedaling around the countryside. For these occasions, he has a car with a neato bike rack on top (see "Transporting You and Your Bike"). He flips the bike up onto the rack, straps it down, then drives up to Cold Rapids and takes a quick loop on the Old Cold Rapids Highway, the Park Road, and the grueling stretch of the Last Chance Road (look at those squiggles through the mountains) back to where he left the car at Cold Rapids. He then drives back to Burgville, ready for work or whatever obligation was cutting his riding time short.

For a treat, Freddy sometimes takes Beula Ashta, his ravishing girl friend, for an unusual day of cycling through the state park on Verde Island out on Lake Wuzblue. They put their bikes on Freddy's car-top carrier and drive the River Road most of the way to King's Beach. They stop along the river somewhere, take the bikes off the car, and ride the last couple of easy, scenic miles to the beach. Then they take the ferry out to Verde Island, where there are beautiful, car-free roads, and ride a few more miles, maybe stopping for a picnic along the way. Towards evening, they take the ferry back to the mainland, pedal back up the River Road to Freddy's car, and drive home. Although not everybody has a handy Verde Island they can take a ferry out to, most of us can find a park within driving distance where there are pleasant, quiet cycling trails or park access roads.

There are times when Freddy feels like cycling a long way in a day, but without taking in too many challenging mountain assaults. For this kind of mood, Freddy has reserved in his repertoire of rides a long, meandering loop to Wuzblue Heights and back. He sweats over the hills on Bart Road to the Old Cold Rapids Highway, then settles into an easy, stretched-out pace for a long, fairly level ramble down to Wuzblue Heights, then he turns east on the Podunk Road to Simms Road, then south on Simms to Kutt Corners, where he turns right on Kutt Road and rides into Long Beach. He follows Highway 40 along the lake to the River Road, then pedals up the river to Burgville. The ride is about 75 miles in length, but never too strenuous. The only things that Freddy has to watch out for on such rides are the wind blowing off the lake in the afternoon, and the traffic on Highway 40, which can be heavy and bothersome on summer weekends.

Over a long weekend, or during a vacation, Freddy sometimes decides to really cut loose and go for a two or three day jaunt on his bike. Sometimes he even goes for longer stints. When he gets the wanderlust, the urge to be completely on the loose with his bike, he first plans what his route is going to be, and what he is going to need to ride that route.

There are two fundamentally different types of trip. One is the classic sort of bike touring, wherein riders take very little with them, and stay in hostels, motels, or hotels, and eat in restaurants or picnic out of saddle bags. This is far and away the simplest kind of touring, and the easiest on the cyclist, because he has to take so little extra weight. But the route must be chosen with your needs in mind. There must be frequent eating and sleeping places along the way. You also have to carry a significant wad of dough to make up for all the other equipment you avoid carrying. To keep expenses down, Freddy belongs to the American Youth Hostels, Inc. (see Addresses) and tries to take tours where there are hostels. This is much easier in the eastern and southern states than in the midwest or the west, where the hostels are few and far between. Another money-saving device that Freddy uses is friendship. He has an arrangement with a number of friends spread around the map, whereby they exchange sleep-over privileges. This makes for inexpensive and convivial touring. "A good friend'll go you a lot farther than a dollar," an old phrase from the hospital South says.

A second kind of touring involves cycle-camping, which can be great fun if you like camping and are willing to carry a fair-sized load on your bike. I'm not. But let's say Freddy is. He plans his route very carefully, using not only maps with the degree of detail

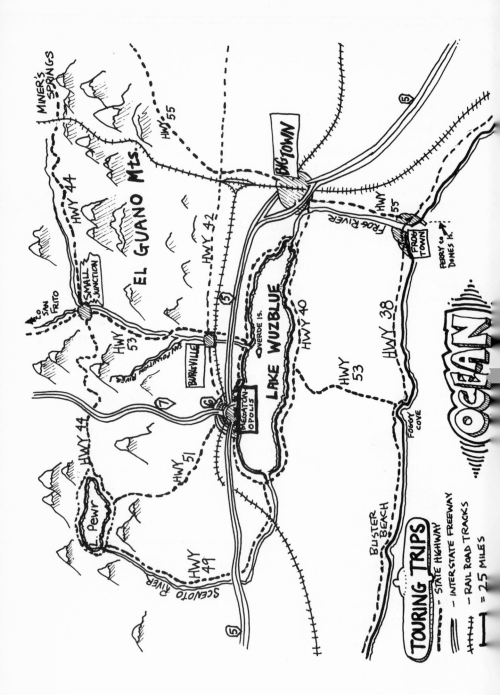

TOURING TRIPS

- - - = STATE HIGHWAY
= INTERSTATE FREEWAY
+++++ = RAIL ROAD TRACKS
— = 25 MILES

MINER'S SPRINGS

HWY 55

BIGTOWN

EL GUANO Mts.

HWY 44

HWY 42

HWY 55

FROG RIVER

FROG TOWN

FERRY to DONES Is.

SMALL JUNCTION

to SAN FRITO

HWY 53

BURKSVILLE

HWY 40

HWY 38

LAKE WUZBLUE

VERDE IS.

FOGGY COVE

HWY 53

MEGALTON OPOLIS

HWY 51

HWY 44

L. PEWR

HWY 49

SCENOTO RIVER

BUSTER BEACH

OCEAN

of the Touring Trips map, but also maps with the degree of detail of the Short Country Trips map. This way, he can see not only the over-all trip route, but also the all-important small roads that parallel the highways, and offer more peaceful, scenic riding. The AAA maps are ideal for the purpose. Topo maps are good, but you have to get an awful lot of them, because each one covers little territory (see Addresses). While planning a trip, Fred finds all the available campsites, and checks them out to see if they will be open and have vacancies. Freddy once saved a little bread, in fact, quite a bit of bread, and bought an extra-light sleeping bag, like a three-pound or less down-filled one of some quality, and alpine cooking and weather-protection gear. That way, he doesn't have to carry any more dead weight than necessary. For all liquids, he uses the feeder bottles like the racers have, that can be bracketed to the bike frame in a number of places.

On the Touring Trips map, some of the areas that might be good for long trips are the ocean coast, the long circuit around Lake Wuzblue, a shorter loop around Lake Pewr, a trip along Highway 44 from Miner's Springs to Lake Pewr, or the scenic downhill ramble from Lake Pewr south along the Scenoto River to Lake Wuzblue.

On the ocean coast ride, especially on summer weekends, traffic might be a problem. Freddy would therefore try to do the bulk of the riding in the morning, and look for side roads paralleling the highway. Also he would determine the prevailing wind direction along the coast (see "Getting on with the Elements") and try to ride most of the time with the wind at his back. There will be plenty of eating and sleeping accommodations along the shore, so Freddy can take a classical type tour if he has the bread.

The same sort of tour can be taken around Lake Wuzblue. Here a major problem is getting through the city areas—Megatonopolis and Bigtown. Freddy would do well to call the Chambers of Commerce in both towns to see if there are any bike trails or suggested bike routes. Some thoughtful cities, like Chicago, have gone to the trouble of making bike trails along their lake shores. But if the route isn't so easy as that, Freddy may have to plan the tour in such a way that he can ride through town early on a weekend morning, sticking to the lesser used side streets and two-way streets without synchronized stoplights and fast traffic.

For a shorter lake loop trip, Freddy can pedal around Lake Pewr, up in the Guano Mountains. The air up there is clear and brisk, the traffic lighter except on summer weekends, and the ride has some exhilarating hill climbs and downhill runs. Freddy can stay at either motels or campsites, or at hostels if there are any. Interesting side trips can be taken up into the mountains around the lake, either hiking or cycling.

For a longer, tougher mountain tour, Freddy can ride on the train with his bike to Miner's Springs, then cycle on Highway 44 from Miner's Springs all the way to Lake Pewr. The ride has lots of ups and downs, so Freddy can't plan on making nearly as many miles a day, but he can find campsites and/or hostels and motels all along the route. He should try to keep his load light and make sure he is in good shape before he starts such a trip, though. Slogging over hill after hill can be miserable if you are in bad shape. Twiddling up the hills at good rpm and zooming downhill can be fun if you're in decent shape.

A great group tour can be taken down Highway 49 from Lake Pewr to Lake Wuzblue. The route is little used, because it is parallel to Highway 51, and 51 is a much quicker way for cars to get from Megatonopolis to Lake Pewr. But the Scenoto River Valley offers some great views, and the ride is mostly downhill, so any rider with a decent bike and a little experience can go along. The only problem with rides like the Scenoto River tour is that they require a driver to take all the riders up to Lake Pewr, and then pick them up down by Lake Wuzblue. A "sag wagon," which follows the cycle route, and picks up tired riders or broken bikes, is a nice thing to have on such a group tour, but then someone has to have the not-so-interesting job of driving along the route at a cyclist's pace. Loop trips have the advantage of bringing the riders back to their cars, where they left them to start the ride. Then there are those rare rides like the one that starts at Miner's Springs, which are reachable by rail. Riding uphill on a train and downhill on a bike is probably an almost ideal combination, but hard to find.

12 THE ROAD-RACING TRIP

Let's keep things straight. I'm not a road racer. I have ridden with a number of decent road racers and even track racers on their training rides, and will tell you what I know about how they get into shape. If you want to race, there are a number of much more knowledgeable books than mine which will tell you about racing tactics and technique. Try the book put out by C.O.N.I., the Central Sports School of Rome, Italy, *Cycling,* for a start. You can get it and other racing books from Books About Cycling, Inc. (see Addresses).

If you want to race, though, you can do a simple test on yourself to see if you're up to doing it right. Try riding 25 miles a day, every day, for a week. Then try riding 35 miles a day for another week. Then try a week of riding 35 miles a day in less than one hour and 45 minutes each trip. That's averaging about twenty miles an hour, which is slow for most road races. If you like riding twenty miles an hour for an hour and 45 minutes every day, with that little a build-up, and if you like the whole process of working up speed, then join the A.B.L.A., the Amateur Bicycling League of America, and learn the rules. Make friends with some racers and ride with them to build up your sprint speed as well as your endurance, start doing intervals on a track or smooth road (intervals are alternate periods of all-out sprinting and easier riding), keep a daily record of your riding time, distance, and how you feel, get a bike that's good for the kind of racing you like, and plan to do lots and lots of riding before you ever win a race.

For the rest of us, the road racing trip is significant in that we can use some of the racer's methods to keep in good physical condition. Eddy Merkx, "Fast Eddy" as he is known in some circles, has won a lot of races. His basic training rule is a good one. Ride lots. Every day. That's how he does it. Now, we can't all trip out on a 50-miler or a "century" every single day, but if we get in a good two or three hour ride two or three times a week, we'll never slump to the point where a good two or three hour ride is no fun. See? To enjoy cycling, you have to do it steadily. It's like riding over hard-packed sand on the beach. If you keep moving, you can do it. But if you slow down, it gets harder and harder, and if you stop altogether, it's really a pain to get going again. Sometimes, admittedly, you just don't feel like riding. But if you can get over your inertia and just get rolling, the enjoyment will come by itself.

Commuting is good regular exercise, of course, if it's convenient, and the weather isn't too rough. There is no substitute, though, for a good two hour jaunt on a quick, light bike. Slogging along to and from work will keep you at a sort of low plateau of fitness, but you need the exhilaration, the uphill spurts, and the fast downhill runs of a good country escape trip to get the old red corpuscles jumping around in there and saying "Whoopie!" A word of warning for people with circulatory problems. Do keep a lid on the red corpuscles' whoopie. They tend to want to break out at the seams if you overdo. And it's easy to overdo on a bike, because you aren't bouncing along uncomfortably like a jogger. You are in a smooth escalation of energy expenditure, imperceptibly nearing your popping point. So take a breather if you start feeling your pulse hammering at the temples. Good, steady cycling is one of the best types of therapy for all kinds of circulatory, as well as orthopedic problems. But take it smooth and easy.

You people who are pressed for time, try taking a sort of mini-interval trip during your lunch hour or maybe even on the way home from work on your commuting bike. Start out at a normal pace and go until you have warmed up a bit, then do an imaginary "jump" or spurt of speed, and pass a whole imagined peleton of Masis and Holdsworths on your trusty Schwinn three speed. You may look a little funny to other people on the street, pedaling along at a mad 100 rpm clip with fenders flapping and no opposition in sight, but what the hell, we all have a little Walter Mitty in us to let out. And in this case, there is nothing wrong with letting off steam by getting into that kind of a trip. It is, after all, only a reduced version of the training technique that builds up the lungs, circulatory systems, and muscles of the racers. Just don't get so far into your imaginary jump that you blow a gasket or an anterior cerebral artery or something.

During the winter weather, cyclists are often forced to curtail or give up their bike trips altogether. Some road racers and many track racers have a way to beat the weather. If you miss your pedaling exercise in the winter, and don't mind putting down a little cash, you can cycle all year round on rollers like the racers use. These professional rollers are not to be confused with exercycles, or those clumsy attachments you stick your back wheel in. Good rollers come in sets of three, on an adjustable rack. You set the rear wheel of your bike between the two close-set rollers, then adjust the third roller, the one that is belt-driven, to the place where it is directly under your front wheel.

It's easiest to learn how to ride on rollers using a fixed gear track bike, but once you get the hang of it, a ten speed will work fine. Get on the bike with something, or better, someone nearby to keep you up. Once you get going, you can balance just as you would normally. But keep steady. Have someone hold the seat post when you are first learning. Make yourself stare

Bike on rollers

at an imaginary point ten feet in front of you instead
of looking down at the rollers. It takes a while to
attain the smoothness and steady balance necessary,
but after a few scary attempts, it becomes completely
natural. Some people I know watch TV while they do
it. The irony of such a thing. If you do get distracted
by TV or something and come off the ends of the
rollers, simply stop pedaling. You don't take off as
you'd expect. Just to be on the safe side, though, don't
ride on rollers around furniture with pointy corners,
or little children. That way, if you lose your balance,
you can fall away from the rollers and not hurt
anything.

Training or keeping in shape on rollers can be as interesting as your imagination makes it. You can work up all kinds of variations of intervals, mini-intervals, short sprints, slow build-ups to high rpm, or long periods of easy-paced pedaling. You'll find that after a while your mind wanders, especially if you are cruising along at an even place. A strange euphoria sets in, and it can turn into quite an unusual trip after all. Don't fall asleep and ride off the ends of the rollers, though.

Whatever training techniques you choose, do spend some of the time at high rpm on the rollers. The more time you spend at high rpm, the more coordination you'll develop. Making nice, smooth, powerful circles with your feet is hard. It's hard enough to draw a nice circle with your hand. If you describe thousands and thousands of circles with your feet as part of your winter keeping-in-shape, you will be able to pedal with less wasted and misdirected energy in the spring. Work on smoothness at high rpm. If you want to, you can even try to develop your ankling a little. But that smooth, fast circle is the first thing. The ankling will come later, by itself.

13 BIKE TRIPS FOR THE FANATIC FRINGE

The following is a compendium of freak-outs for those who can a) stand the physical and mental abuse that are inherent in each trip, b) afford buying and replacing the equipment required and often used up or broken, c) find sources for the equipment, and places to do the various trips.

FIXING UP AND RIDING A HIGH-WHEELER

The old Ordinaries or "Penny-farthing" bikes that were used in the late 1800s (when the only way they could make a bike go faster was to make its power wheel bigger) are rare these days. If you can get one with a big wheel and a frame (or "backbone") that are in decent shape, you can restore the rest of the parts, or for a bit of bread, have them machined. Use wheelchair "cab" rubber for the tires, and have the tire mounting done by either a wheelchair company, or a big, old bike shop with the experience and the wire-tightening machine necessary. There are expert restorers like Al Kaiser of Santa Rosa, California, dotted around the country, and you might try to locate the nearest high-wheeler freak by asking the bike shops or the League of American Wheelmen representative in your area.

The wheels on high-wheelers can be trued like any bike wheel, but go easy. Old spokes are weak. New spokes can be made from wire. Get nipples from a wheelchair, then match the wire gauge and the necessary threading die to the nipple. Modern cranks and pedals can be adapted to the old wheel. Bearings are a problem. The balls themselves can be replaced, of course, but if the races are all pitted and worn, there's not much you can do short of having a machinist remake them.

As for the seat, the most commonly missing or
ruined item, you can stretch and rivet new leather, if
you have the old hardware, or you can attach a regular
new bike seat to the frame with two "U" bolts of the
one and one-quarter inch size that they use to hold
exhaust pipes to car frames. Leave the seatpost clamp
of the new seat in place, with a sawed-off section of
seatpost in it. You can move the clamp towards the
back of the seat and use it for a block to hold the back
of the seat higher off the curved frame than the front,
thus making it level.

When you get the thing all restored, you can try to
ride it. Good luck. Find an empty parking lot or school
ground to make your first attempts in.

The trick to getting on and off that seat way up in the air is to do it slowly. That's how I learned from Al Kaiser, a real pro at the art. It is easiest to use a slight downhill slope, where you can coast along as you get your balance. Start by standing behind the bike, with both hands gripping the handle grips at the ends of the handlebars. Then put the edge of the toe of your left shoe on the bracket that sticks out on the left side of the bike frame. (If the bracket sticks out on the right side, put your right foot in place.) Keep your knee tucked back and to the side, out of the path that big wheel will take if you turn to the right. With your weight on your left foot, hop along on your right foot as if you are pedaling a giant scooter. Do that until you get the idea of how to balance the thing, then pull yourself up until you are standing straight on your left foot. Reach your right foot forward, and begin pedaling with just that one foot. Noodle along like that for a while, standing on your left foot, and pedaling with your right, until you feel fairly secure. Then, as the right foot is pushing the pedal down, raise yourself onto the seat with your arms. Don't leap from the foot bracket— you'd be in danger of going right over the front. "Taking a header" as it is known, which is literally what you do. Right on your face. So lift yourself into the saddle slow and easy. Once you are in place, try to keep the thing going at a fair clip—say five miles an hour—it'll be easier to balance at that speed for a start. Whenever you make a turn, remember that the big wheel will pivot out from under the frame and tend to hit your leg. Wear tight pants so they don't flap around and get caught, and if you are making a sharp turn, stick the outside leg away from the bike and pedal with one foot, to keep things clear of each other. *Don't* ride down a steep hill until you are very experienced at riding the high-wheeler. In fact, avoid all situations where you might have to make a sudden stop. If you ever slam on the brake that stops the front wheel, you will be sure to take a header.

To dismount, get the bike going at a fair clip, so that it will coast as you go through the process. Reach back with your left foot and find the bracket back there. Hard to find, isn't it? You'd swear someone took it off while you were riding. But don't look back there to find it. Search around with your left toe until you do. Then lift yourself off the saddle, still pedaling with your right foot. When your weight is all on your left toe, you can put on the brake, and step down as the bike slows to a stop. Whew! You can stop shaking now.

If you get in trouble at any point of the mounting or dismounting process, or while riding, hold down your urge to get off on the side by putting your foot down as on a regular two-wheeler. If you let the high-wheeler tip all the way over to one side, you will come down very hard on that one foot. Always exit to the rear of the bike, even if you just push yourself back off the seat and slide ingloriously down the frame. That's better than either the front or side exit.

For the real fanatic and master of Ordinary riding, there are long-distance rides on the high-wheeler. They are incredibly arduous. The bikes weigh between 40 and 70 pounds, and are incapable of going up steep hills even with a superman pedaling. Downhill stretches are dangerous, to say the least. Stories are told of red-hot brake spoons, and nerves shattering under the stress.

Whatever you do with a high-wheeler, do treat it with care and respect for its age. The metallurgy in the 1880s wasn't too advanced, and the metal hasn't gotten any stronger with age.

To keep your venerable old bike in as good shape as possible, it's a good idea to nickel plate the parts that were nickel or silver plated originally (they didn't have chrome in those days). This includes all the parts of the headset. The job is expensive, but will add to the life of those irreplaceable parts. Paint the rest of the bike with several coats of black lacquer, hand-rubbing with very fine emery paper between coats.

LIVING ON YOUR BIKE

There's a whole world out there waiting to be ridden around in (on a normal bike, we're talking about now). And you don't have to have a terrific amount of cycling muscle or money to get around in it. You just have to be able to cut loose, and then stick to your guns and buck up under the difficulties that befall anybody who lives on the road. It takes guts. And the ability to adapt to whatever conditions and people you run into.

Before you go, you should try to get a good bike together, to limit the number of mechanical problems that you'll have on the road. You want a light, limber, strong bike. One made with double-butted tubing will be the best, with a long design (see Al Eisentraut's frame design discussion). Low gears are a must unless you are a super strong rider. A 40 tooth small chainwheel, or even smaller, is a good idea, and a 26 tooth large sprocket on the freewheel, or even larger if you have a derailleur that can handle the range.

Make sure the wheels are built to last. That means spending some extra money, but it will be well worth it. Get high-quality, low-flange hubs. The sealed bearing type is the best. Have the wheels spoked with double-butted stainless steel or rustless spokes, three crossed, and laced (see "Which Bike for You"). You can get a 40 spoke rear wheel rather than the normal 36 for extra strength back there where you need it. Steel rims and clincher tires are more utilitarian than aluminum alloy rims and sew-ups.

Get good carriers that fit the bike properly, both front and back, to distribute the weight. If you can keep the over-all luggage weight under twenty pounds, then you can use the T.A. type carriers. But if you are going to be carrying lots of weight, you'll have to get something like the Rene Herse carrier frames, or maybe one of the new tote-trailers. These are hard to find. Try the mail order catalogues, like Big Wheel or Cyclopedia (see Addresses). Mount standard bags that fit on the carriers. Then work like hell to keep your luggage weight under 35 pounds. Get a down-filled nylon sleeping bag, a super light tube tent, and alpine cooking equipment. Use light water bottles, like the racers use, to carry all fluids. Get by with the minimum number of tools—a crescent wrench, a little screwdriver like the Singer sewing machine ones, a freewheel remover, a chain tool, two tire irons, a patch kit and pump, and a pair of pliers with wire clippers incorporated. Make sure each tool is of high quality so that it will last.

As for parts, you can't be prepared for everything. Take some cables, both brake and derailleur, and a number of links of chain. You might have to get a whole new chain at some point on your journey, because that kind of riding is hard on chains, and riding with a loose chain is hard on you. But that can be done at a city where there is a big bike shop. The same goes for tires. Change them while you're in a town, before they get too thin, but don't bother with carrying a spare around with you all the time. Just carry tubes. When you buy tires and chains, don't try to save money. Even if it cuts into your food money. Good tires, like the high pressure gum-wall ones, are worth their weight in gold.

When your bike is set up, ride it for a while around your home before you take off. Ride it fully loaded to get the feel of how it handles. Build up your strength to take on the extra load. Try out different clothes, and choose the lightest possible, like a sweat shirt and a nylon windbreaker, and cut-off sweat pants (comfy!) or racing tights, and minimum dress-up clothes.

As you travel, try to plan ahead. Map out each day's route ahead of time, even if you don't plan on sticking to the route. Wandering is nice, but you have to keep in mind that by the end of the day you are going to be hungry and tired. Perhaps the nicest thing about such tripping is the people you meet when you aren't so well organized, the people who share food, shelter, and troubles with you. It's always amazing how many decent folk there are. Of course, there are a lot of others you have to put up with too. But that's part of the bag. One trick you can try if you can't afford or find a camping place is to use the nearest graveyard. You won't be bothered there, unless you are prejudiced against ghosts. If you find a handy mausoleum to hide behind, so much the better. Some trip.

While on the road, always remember that wise riding maxim, tend to your needs before they are imminent. Eat before you are hungry, drink before you're thirsty, shift down before you get to a hill, check the brakes before a downhill grade, and go to the john before you're uncomfortable.

Living on your bike is much nicer with a friend, unless you are the loner type. You may argue with your friend a lot, but there will be times that you'll be awfully thankful for his help and different point of view.

BEACH RIDING

This type of cycling is for dispensible balloon-tire bikes only. The beach is the trashmo's turf. Sand and water, especially salt water, do their work on a bike's innards. No beach bike can be expected to last more than a summer or two. So get a cheap clunker for a few bucks from a tag sale, a garage sale, a rummage sale, or the local flea market, then feel free to run it into the ground.

Beach riding requires no great skill or mental power. The harder you go at it, though, the more fun you seem to have. Try going down to the beach at a spring low tide and just torch around on the hard-packed sand that has been bared by the receding water. You may find that the sand isn't too hard-packed. If so, try later. Sand consistencies change depending on wave and weather conditions. On good, hard sand, you can ride fast enough to do long side-slipping skids, spin-outs, wheelies, hookers, and a lot of other foolishness. For a change, ride down near the water's edge, and dodge the swash as it sweeps up with the wave's last energy. Cut across an occasional tongue of the swash at high speed. Water will pinwheel all over you. Now you're starting to get into it. Make a little ski jump by piling sand up to form an incline, and laying a plank on top, then go flying. Or zoom over a cusp and land in a tide pool. Yeah, and for a grand finale, wind up the old trashmo to about 120 rpm on the hard-pack, and head right into the maw of a five foot comber. Hooooy! Beach riding is best done in swimming attire, on a warm day. But if you work up enough of a sweat at the hard-pack show, the finale can be fun anytime. You wind up pedaling through the bounding main in slow motion, with the sea-weed billowing over your knees.

If you want the bike to last at all with that kind of treatment, keep oil or even grease on the chain at all times, and squirt lots of oil into the wheel, bottom bracket, and headset bearings as well. It's often amazing how long the old crate will put up with it. Especially if it's one of those great old Schwinns.

ICE RIDING

In the same hair-brained, childishly joyous vein as beach riding is ice riding. For those of you who live nearer northern lakes than southern beaches, you might give it a try. Again, the bike should be a cheap old one speed balloon-tire bomber. Try to get one with a good, tight-fitting back tire, or buy a heavy-duty nobby tire for the purpose. Take your chosen back tire off the wheel, and take the tube out. Hammer roofing tacks from the inside of the tire out through the casing and the thickest part of the rubber, right through the nobs if it's a nobby tire. When the tacks stick out, grab them with pliers and pull them until the wide head of each tack is flush against the inner side of the tire. Then cut off the end of each tack with clippers, so that only about a quarter of an inch is sticking out of the rubber. Replace the regular tube with a thorn-proof tube to slow down the puncture rate. Fill the tire with a good deal of pressure, up to 45 pounds if it'll take it. With a short nail sticking out of the tire every inch or so all around the tire, you can get something like traction on the ice. Nails also help on the front tire, but you don't need so many, and you needn't get a special tube and tire, because the weight and torque are not such a factor.

119

With or without nails, riding on ice is crazy. You can always seem to get going if you keep at it, but the trouble develops when you try to stop or turn suddenly. Wear plenty of heavy clothing to pad your falls, and don't try ice riding at all if you have brittle bones. You can have fun cutting in and out of patches of powder snow, throwing the stuff all over the place, or there's always the old full-speed-into-the-snowdrift bit, but be on the lookout for hidden rocks or hard-packed base snow. Also, steer clear of skaters and other pedestrians. You are much less in control than either you or they might expect.

THE DIRT ROAD TRIP

If you like hiking out away from the crowd, and seeing lots of wildlife that stays away from the crowd, and if you have a bike that is sturdy and limber, you might try riding on some of the lesser used or even abandoned backroads in your vicinity. Make sure that you are riding where it is safe and legal, though. Park roads are the best bet (see the Park Road along the west fork of the San Polluto River on the Short Country Trips map). Often the roads used by park personnel for maintenance are deserted, scenic, and convenient for use by cyclists. Private farm roads, lumber roads, or mountain fire trails are riskier. It's best to ride only where you are known, or where you are familiar enough with the locals that they won't think of you as a threatening trespasser. Take care of a few social amenities, and get to know a few of the local property owners before you go through a road that's new to you, and you'll find that your reception will be a lot better. Don't take a whole crowd of your friends when you go cycling through private land. Somehow, landowners feel much more harassed by groups of trespassers. The owners are often out there for the solitude, after all.

Whenever you take a backroad trip of any length, take a spare tire, or a tube and irons and a patch kit for clinchers, and leave word with someone at home as to your planned route and time of return. People have been known to get hopelessly lost cycling within ten miles of their homes. Wear bright orange or yellow clothing while out in the rough, and don't ride during the hunting season, for obvious reasons.

CYCLO CROSS

Cyclo cross riding is the outermost frontier of the bicycle trip. It is not like moto cross racing on motorcycles, where there is usually a course laid out that is something close to possible. There have been cyclo cross races on courses through which some of the riders could stay aboard the bike, but those weren't serious cyclo cross races. The idea of the cyclo cross race and cyclo cross tripping for fun is to find the most difficult and challenging route from point A to point B. When you are partaking of the sport on your own, you can make it as difficult as you want. The race courses often involve negotiating cliffs, hedges, roaring creeks, ice, mud, and other natural obstacles. There is a point at which the trip becomes idiocy, even for a hardened veteran. And it is always extremely debilitating for both rider and bike.

There are two approaches to equipment for cyclo cross. One is to use an old, decrepit bike with cheap parts and basic arrangements like one gear, foot brakes, and old clincher tires. This system often produces short rides. The advantage to it is that the bike always gives out before the rider. The other route is to use a fancy or especially adapted bike with things like chain guides attached to the chainwheels, nobby sew-ups, and a super-springy frame with a high bottom bracket. Bikes like these are a lot more common in England, the muddy home of the cyclo cross, than they are in America. Compromises often work fairly well, but no bike, no matter how strong, can stand up under the punishment for long. To say nothing of the rider.

The fun of the sport, on the other hand, is the supreme test it is not only of your and the bike's endurance, but of your combined abilities. A great bike with an experienced rider can do amazing things in the rough. And the feeling you get, with the bike springing and flexing and responding to all the natural unevenness of the terrain—that feeling is incomparable. A little like sailing a fine racing boat in rough seas. Or going fast in a Porsche on a winding mountain road. But a good deal safer than either. You can feel your bike and yourself doing the best possible under stress without seriously endangering life or limb.

There are, however, numerous pitfalls to the cyclo cross trip. Like cliffs and roaring creeks. Learn to watch not only the ground in front of you, but also that a few yards ahead, to avoid crashes and cold swims. Wear long pants, or knickers and knee socks, and long-sleeve shirts to avoid brambles, poison oak, or poison ivy. If you live in cattle or dairy country, watch out for the herd, and try not to divide it; panicky cows are utterly stupid, and capable of running right over you. If you are using sew-ups, stay clear of cactus, berry vines, and fields with burrs during the dry summer and fall months. Sew-ups hold up very well under all kinds of rock-pounding, log-jumping, and general slamming around, but just let one little patch of burrs go under the wheels, and you will be doing the seamstress and patch-man trip for weeks.

Learn to psyche out the ground hardness, and what kind of traction you are heading into. On sandy or deep-dusty trails, stick to the high side, the uphill side of the rut. Keep looking for hard-packed strips or flat areas with short grass growing. Keep your speed and your rpms up, so you can make it from one better-traction area to the next. In the mud, ride in a low gear, and keep the rpms way up. Stay on the high spots, out of the muddy puddles and low bogs, as much as possible. Again, pick out the flat areas with short grass growing on them. Steer around high clumps of grass at all times. They can hide stumps, boulders, pot-holes, or meadow-muffins, if you're in Marlboro country.

On hardpan roads strewn with loose sand or gravel, you can go at a fair clip, if you only make small correctional maneuvers. In other words, don't ever brake hard, or lean into a corner hard, or pedal too hard. This riding requires constant planning ahead, so that you can make a curve into a series of slight turns, or build up speed before you get to a hill-climb and slow down before a steep downhill. With even the best technique, you'll only feel half in control a lot of the time on sandy or gravelly surfaces. But just keep your cool, and try to keep the front wheel in front, with lots of little corrections instead of big sloppy ones, and you'll be astounded at what you can pull through.

When going down steep grades on slippery surfaces, you'll notice that the back wheel tends to skid and slip as you go over bumps. This is because your weight shifts forward in that situation, making the front wheel's traction better than that of the back wheel. To even things out, sit far back on the seat, and make the front brake do more of the braking work.

Negotiate rocky creek beds or slides slowly. Get into your lowest gear. Lift up on the front wheel whenever it is going over a rock, tree-limb, or other obstacle, then lean down on it so the back wheel will trail over easily. Don't ever get so wrapped up in what the wheels are doing that you forget about your overhead clearance, though. Your head will be the first thing to hit a low limb or rock overhang.

When you have to portage over boulders or logs, pick up the bike from the left side. Stick your right arm through the diamond of the frame. Let the top tube rest on your right shoulder, and grab the handlebars with your right hand. That will leave your left hand free for balance.

Sometimes the greatest part of the cyclo cross trip is when you aren't doing it. If you have been pushing along through the wilderness for half an hour, straining and concentrating completely on what you are doing, then stop still for a breather, the peacefulness of it all comes home clearer than it ever would otherwise. And you can be just as sure you won't be disturbed as you are sure that you aren't spoiling any of the things that make it nice out there. A nice trip.

14 THE FRAME

by ALBERT EISENTRAUT, Frame Builder

Bicycle frames are available from many sources. The design of frames may vary from builder to builder, or from country to country, or even from one period of time to another within the work of one builder. The majority of frames in common use are designed for multi-purpose or all-purpose application. But because of the wide range of frame designs that are suitable for any single application, and because of differences in the availability of specific frame types in different areas, futile arguments arise as to what any particular frame is "designed to do" and whether a rider is using the one frame that is "perfect for himself." If a rider is entirely happy with the performance of his bike, taking into consideration the conditions under which he uses it, there is little more one can say. Why argue with success?

In most instances the satisfied rider has simply become accustomed to an available design, and is making the best of its peculiarities. Seldom is it possible to try out enough different bicycle frames under enough different conditions to make a logical frame choice. There are also many psychological factors involved in the choosing of a bike that aren't relevant to the design or the ridability of the frame at all. I am very hesitant to make absolute statements about frame design, simply because as soon as I do, someone will respond by saying, "So and so did this or won that on a frame that was not what Albert Eisentraut recommended." This just reinforces the idea that there is a wide range of possible solutions to any frame designing problem, and any solution might work well for a rider who is accustomed to it. Besides, in any success-

ful cycling activity, the frame is only part of the phenomenon. Physical ability, psychology, other equipment on the bike, and the nature of the activity itself
all have to be considered. Keeping all of the complica-
tions above in mind, however, general statements can
still be made about frame construction that will aid
the rider in selecting a good frame for a particular
activity.

Before considering the application of any frame,
though, one must understand more about the mate-
rials, design, and construction techniques that create
the finished product.

TUBES

A bike frame and fork function together as a unit.
They are made of various tubular members, each of
which is carefully designed and formed for its particular role.

The members of cheaper frames consist of seamed,
resistance-welded tubes. The tensile strength (yield) of
these tubes can be as low as 45,000 pounds per square
inch. That might appear to be a great deal of stress
required to pull the metal apart, but in comparison to
the finer grades of steel tubing, the seamed tubes are
functionally weak. Because of the low strength,
thicker-walled tubing must be used. A frame built
with this tubing is heavy and gives a very dull and
unresponsive feeling to the rider.

The frames of medium-priced bikes use seamless
straight gauge tubing. This tubing is usually made of
relatively low-carbon steel, which has a tensile strength
of around 60,000 pounds per square inch. Bikes made
with this type of tubing are somewhat lighter than
seamed-tubing ones, and can be quite ridable with
adequate frame design.

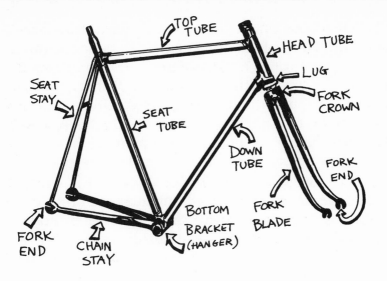

The best frames utilize high-carbon, cold-drawn seamless steel tubes with very thin walls. They are much lighter and stronger than the others, and give a definite feeling of life and responsiveness to the rider. The steel used, for example, in Reynolds 531 tubing has a composition which includes:

.23%—.29% carbon
1.25%—1.45% manganese
.15%—.25% molybdenum
.15%—.35% silicon
.045% sulfur (maximum)
.045% phosphorus (maximum)

The tubing has a minimum tensile strength of approximately 90,000 pounds per square inch before brazing, and a minimum tensile strength of 80,000 psi after brazing. It may be straight gauge, or butted.

Straight gauge tubes begin as solid bar ingots, which are penetrated through the middle while still hot. The resulting crude tube is annealed and pickled for the proper softness and a smooth finish. One end of the tube is hammered closed to make a point, then the tube is cold drawn. A "mandrel" or accurately shaped bar is placed inside the tube, then it is pulled with great force through a succession of dies which squeeze the tube to exactly the right outside diameter and wall thickness around the mandrel.

Butted tubes are those which have thicker walls at the ends than in the middle (see the tubing illustration). The butted contour is attained by starting with a straight gauge tube that is slightly greater in overall or outside diameter and wall thickness than that which is desired. A mandrel with a shape and size exactly like that required for the final butted contour is placed inside the oversized tube. The tube and mandrel are then both drawn repeatedly with great force through a die or hole which squeezes and narrows the tube to the proper outside diameter and inside contour around the mandrel. The tube is then passed through a constricting space between two inclined rollers, which action momentarily springs the diameter of the tube to a size greater than natural. At the instant that the tube is wide enough to go around the mandrel, the mandrel is drawn out, and the tube is allowed to spring back to its final form. As is shown in the illustration, one butted end of each tube is always longer than the other. This allows the frame builder to cut off part of

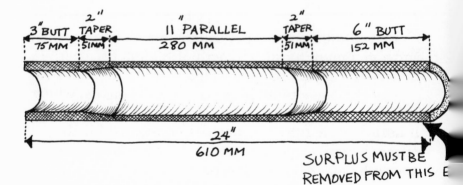

that end to get the size needed without removing all the butted section of the tube.

The value of butted tubes is their combined strength and lightness. The stresses on any bike frame are concentrated at the joints. Therefore, the ends of the tubes need more strength than the middles. Also, in brazing, the joints are subjected to heat that can weaken the tubing. The heavier gauge of the ends of butted tubes counterbalances the effect of the heat. Finally, in finishing any joint, the frame builder files off flux and excess filler around the edges of the lug. This filing removes a slight amount of steel from the tube, and the thicker ends of butted tubes guard against any resultant weakness.

Nearly all racing and fine touring bikes are made with butted tubing. Some special frames, however, for time trials, record attempts, or pursuit racing (in which long-term durability is of limited importance), are made of extremely light straight gauge tubing.

A number of companies supply quality tubing made expressly for bicycle frames. A few of the more common are Vitus (French), Falck (Italian), Day and Day (Japanese), Mansmann (German), Columbus (Italian), and Reynolds (English). High-strength American Chrome Molybdenum steel tubing is available and used in some frames, but at this time it is not available in a butted form. Reynolds 531 and Columbus have both been used for a number of years, and have earned extremely good reputations for reliability and precision. They are used in the construction of the majority of the world's outstanding frames.

Columbus and Reynolds tubes are generally available as listed on the next two pages. In reading the wall thicknesses shown, one should remember that the lower the gauge number, the thicker a tube's wall will be.

TOP TUBE

Outside diameter of 25.4 mm (used by English or Italian)

Outside diameter of 26 mm (used by French)

Walls butted to gauges:

    21/24 (.032"/.022") by Reynolds

    20/23 (.036"/.024") by Columbus

    19/22 (.040"/.028") by Columbus and Reynolds

Walls straight gauge:

    23 (.024") by Columbus

DOWN TUBE

Outside diameter of 28.6 mm (English or Italian)

Outside diameter of 28 mm (French)

Walls butted to gauges:

    20/23 (.036/.024") by Reynolds or Columbus

    19/22 (.040"/.028") by Reynolds or Columbus

    18/21 (.048"/.032") by Reynolds

Walls straight gauge:

    23 (.024") by Columbus

SEAT TUBE

Outside diameter of 28.6 mm (English or Italian)

Outside diameter of 28 mm (French)

Walls single-butted to gauges:

    21/24 (.032"/.022") by Reynolds

    20/23 (.036"/.024") by Columbus

    19/22 (.040"/.028") by Reynolds or Columbus

Walls straight gauge:

    23 (.024") by Columbus

HEAD TUBE

Outside diameter of 31.75 mm (English or Italian)

Outside diameter of 32 mm (French)

Walls straight gauge:

    20 (.036") by Reynolds or Columbus

    22 (.028") by Reynolds or Columbus

CHAIN STAYS

Outside diameter of 22.2 mm, tapered to 11 mm
(English or Italian)
Outside diameter of 19 mm, tapered to 11 mm (French)
Outside diameter swaged 24 x 22.2 mm, to 12 mm,
by Columbus
Walls straight gauge:
22 (.028") by Reynolds or Columbus
21 (.032") by Reynolds
20 (.036") by Reynolds
19 (.040") by Columbus

SEAT STAYS

Outside diameter of 12.5 mm, 14 mm, or 16 mm, all
tapered to either 9 mm or 10 mm
Walls straight gauge:
22 (.028") by Reynolds or Columbus
20 (.036") by Reynolds or Columbus

FORK BLADES, ROUND

Outside diameter of 22 mm (French, Italian)
Outside diameter of 22.2 mm (English)
Outside diameter of 24 mm (Italian)
Walls taper gauged:
17/22 (.056"/.036") by Reynolds
Walls straight gauge:
19 (.040") by Columbus

FORK BLADES, OVAL

Outside diameter of 22.2 mm shaped to
oval 16 mm x 29 mm
Walls taper gauged:
18/21 (.048"/.036") by Reynolds
OR
Outside diameter of 24 mm shaped to
oval 19 mm x 28 mm

(over)

Walls straight gauge:
  18 (.048") by Columbus
  20 (.036") by Columbus

STEERING COLUMN
Outside diameter of 25 mm (French)
Outside diameter of 25.4 mm (English, Italian)
Walls single-butted to gauge:
  13/16 (.092"/.064") by Reynolds or Columbus
  Columbus steering rifled for added strength

The various tube diameters and wall thicknesses
have specific applications in complete frames. For
instance, the common road bike of Reynolds tubing,
as imported into this country, is equipped with 21/24
gauge top and seat tubes, a 20/23 gauge down tube,
21 gauge chain stays, 14 or 16 mm O.D. 20 gauge seat
stays, and 18/21 gauge oval fork blades. Tubing of
these weights and dimensions makes a good all-purpose
frame that can be used successfully for touring or
racing by a rider who weighs less than 150 pounds, and
who is under six feet tall. Tubing of the above weights
can also be used to build time trial or pursuit frames
for heavier or stronger racers. But it is generally considered too light for use under extreme conditions,
such as criterium racing or extensive steep climbing,
in which a great deal of force is exerted on the frame
by strong competitive riders.

The common road bike built using Columbus tubing
is equipped with "SL" tubing: 20/23 gauge top, down,
and seat tubes, 22 gauge chain stays, 14 mm O.D. 22
gauge seat stays, and 20 gauge fork blades. This frame
is excellent for general-purpose riding or racing by a
rider less than 160 pounds in weight, or for touring by
a stronger or heavier rider. The frame is generally
stiffer than that of the comparable Reynolds tube
bike, and absorbs less of the force placed on it.

Frames larger than 61 cm (24") built of Columbus tubing are supplied with "SP" tubing. They have 19/22 gauge top, down, and seat tubes, 19 gauge chain stays, 14 mm O.D. 20 gauge seat stays, and 18 gauge fork blades. This tubing is well suited for a strong, heavy racer. Frames built with it are also good for a heavier tourist, but may prove to be too harsh for the average rider. Touring frames used for carrying large amounts of weight may use the heavier gauge tubes, but they should be specially designed to eliminate any resulting harshness.

For track racing, the standard all-purpose Reynolds frame is quite usable, especially for the smaller and lighter rider. But increased weight and strength of a rider increases the demands made of the frame, and heavier tubing should be used.

Columbus supplies two types of tubes for track frames, "PS" and "PL". PS tube sets consist of 19/22 gauge top, down, and seat tubes, 24 mm 19 gauge chain stays, 16 mm 20 gauge seat stays, and 24 mm 19 gauge fork blades. PS is the heaviest type of tubing generally available for racing bicycle frames, and is commonly used for sprint and six-day race frames.

PL tubing is comprised of 23 straight gauge tubing, with 22.2 mm 22 gauge chain stays, 14 mm 22 gauge seat stays, and 22 mm 20 gauge fork blades. Its extreme lightness is recommended for use in building pursuit frames.

The only way that one can get variations of the above general patterns of tubes is by having a frame custom made. A custom builder can make combinations of different tubes at will. The finished frame in each case might better suit the needs of a particular rider or a particular event. As will be seen later in this chapter, the custom builder combines special uses of tubing with a specialized frame design to solve an individual's frame problem.

In addition to the above tube types available to the builder, Reynolds and Columbus make super-light tubing especially for record attempts. This tubing is not generally available to just any builder, and seldom finds its way into the United States. It is reported to have wall thicknesses of 25 gauge (.020") or even thinner, and can be used to construct frames which weigh less than three pounds.

Titanium, aluminum and carbon fiber have also been used successfully in building experimental bicycle frames; but each will require improvements in design before it is practical for general use.

FRAME JOINT BONDING

There are only a few ways that the steel tubes of bicycles can be joined. These include welding and brazing, the second of which can be done with or without the aid of lugs, or sleeves, at the joints.

Welding is a metal joining process whereby the tube surfaces are bonded together while molten. It is commonly used on less expensive bikes. Welded frames are suitable for use by children, but have little value for the serious pleasure cyclist, tourist, or racer. They are never used on quality bicycles because welding concentrates all the stress in any joint on one segment of the frame tubing. Light bicycle tubing is not normally thick enough to distribute the stress; if the type of tubing used for quality bikes were to be welded, it would have to be of a wall thickness gauge 12 (.104"). This would make for a very heavy frame. Also, at the point of any weld, there is a change in the crystalline structure of the base metal, and a slight undercutting, which weakens it to such a degree that it is not acceptable for a bike frame.

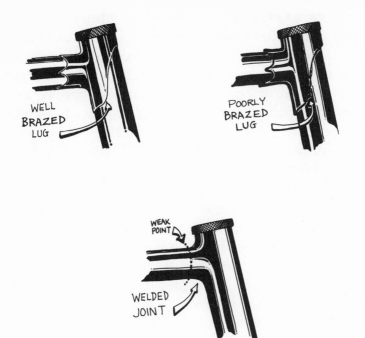

WELL
BRAZED
LUG

POORLY
BRAZED
LUG

WEAK
POINT

WELDED
JOINT

Frame Joints

A much more practical solution to the problem of joining the tubes of a light bike frame is brazing. Brazing is a process which uses a non-iron based "filler" metal that has a melting point much below that of the frame tubes, but above 800 degrees Fahrenheit. The filler metal wets the tubes when it is molten, then flows by capillary action throughout the joint. There is a slight diffusion of the filler into the heated, but solid metal of the tubes, causing a strong, evenly stressed bond.

Different alloy fillers are used for brazing bike frames, the most common of which is soft brass brazing alloy. It has a composition of approximately 59% copper and 30% zinc. It has a relatively high melting point, above 1600 degrees F. But it combines the good qualities of excellent flow characteristics, an adequate ability to form fillets or bands (as needed in lugless construction), and, most important, inexpensive price. Many of the world's quality frame builders use it therefore, in spite of the fact that it requires heating the tubes of the frame to at least 1600 degrees, a heat which can lower the tensile strength of the tubes from 90,000 to 80,000 psi.

Rather than heat the frame tubes to such an extent, some builders prefer bonding frames with silver base brazing alloy, which melts at temperatures near 1200 degrees F. These alloys have flow characteristics even better than those of the brass brazing alloys, but they require very careful cleaning and fluxing (bathing with a chemical agent that removes oxides from the tube's surface, keeps the surface free of oxides during brazing, and aids capillary action through the joint). The silver alloys are up to ten times as expensive as the brass brazing alloys. In the minds of some builders, though, the price is justified by the low melting point; if a silver-brazed bike sustains a bad accident resulting in a crushed tube, for instance, the tube can be replaced easily. It is difficult to melt a brass brazed joint and bond it a second time without seriously affecting the strength of all the tubes at the joint.

Nickel silver brazing alloy can also be used for joining bike frames, especially if lugs are employed, but the great strength of the alloy works against the strength of the joint as a whole, because it creates such a rigid bond.

In lugless frame construction, for instance, the use of nickel bronze alloy fillers creates a joint that is so rigid that the stresses are not distributed, but rather concentrated around the perimeter of the fillet, as the stresses of a welded joint are focused at the edge of the weld. The softer brass alloys are better suited for lugless frame construction because the brass is weaker than the tube metal, though more than strong enough to bond the joint. A brass fillet at a frame joint distributes the stresses evenly between the tubes precisely because it has a slight amount of give. Although lugless joints made with brass alloy are feasible from a structural standpoint, not many bikes are made with them. The method requires that the intersecting tubes be cut with extreme accuracy. The tubes must also be held in a "jig" or stable clamping structure during the extended hand-brazing period. Another drawback to lugless construction is that it requires the use of slightly larger gauge tubes than lug construction, to make up for the slightly inferior stress distribution achieved without lugs. The thicker tubes are heavier, so that the overall weight of the lugless frame is near that of a bike frame made with lugs. Also, aesthetically speaking, a lugged frame is more attractive to most riders.

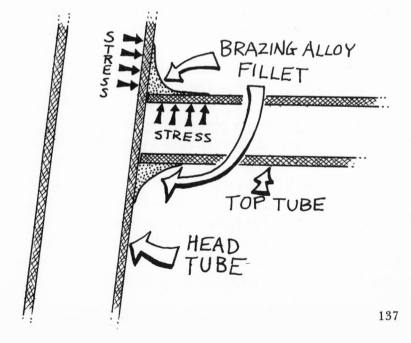

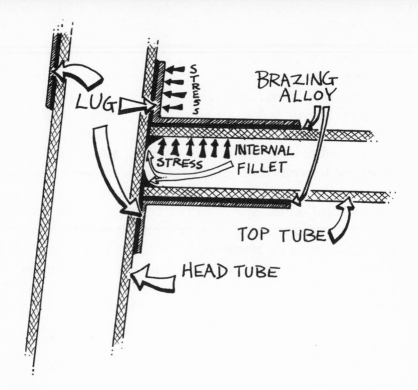

Quality bike frames are therefore usually built with lugs. This method of construction allows on the one hand for very fine precision finishing, or on the other hand for mass production because it is so reliable and flexible. A properly brazed lug distributes stress over the entire area of contact between lug and tubes.

In bonding a lug joint, the builder carefully prepares the tube and lug, insuring the proper clearance between the two; then he cleans and fluxes the area of contact meticulously. He either pins the tubes in place, spot-welds them, or holds the parts in a jig while he heats them to exactly the right temperature for the filler to melt and flow through the joint. In mass production, the brazing may be done by using automatically controlled burners and preplaced alloy. The difference between a skillfully and a poorly brazed joint can be gauged by how long it takes the builder to clean the joint when he is finished. If the craftsman is skilled with a torch and accurate with the brazing alloy, the only clean-up required may be the removal of flux and a slight amount of alloy with a fine file, before the final polishing with abrasive cloth. A poor brazing job may require many hours of hand filing to get a decent result, and even this will often have a worn look nowhere nearly as pleasing or as sound as the crisp, well-brazed joint.

For an exceptionally strong brazed joint, the builder can cut his tubes so that they join very accurately; then he can do a combination of lugless and lugged brazing. Filler alloy is preplaced inside the tubes to be bonded, then a lug is employed. The entire joint is heated to the melting point of the alloy, and filler is made to penetrate from the outside of the joint as well as from the inside. This method requires extra preparation and very proficient brazing technique, but it does produce a joint of maximum strength.

Frame failure is very rare in quality bikes, even with standard lug construction. If there is a failure, it is usually due to one of two types of poor brazing technique. Inadequate cleaning or complete disregard of a joint during the brazing process can cause the joint to have a lack of brazing alloy bonding the frame members and the lug. This construction error occurs almost exclusively in less expensive production bikes, where boredom plays a role in the builders' efficiency. The failure, a parting of tube and lug, usually occurs during the first 500 miles of riding.

Another cause of frame failure is overheating during the brazing process. This causes either an inclusion of the brass alloy, or simply a weakening of the metal of a tube due to change in the crystalline structure. This type of failure often will not develop at all, if the bike is ridden moderately. But under heavy use by a strong and heavy rider, it does sometimes occur.

The style of the lugs used rarely affects the strength of any brazed joint. It is the manner in which the lugs are prepared and finished that is important. Frame lugs are available from several major sources in Europe and Japan. Each supplier produces several different styles, and the relative state of finish varies from company to company. There is only a slight variation between the angles that are available, but this is no problem for the builder, because the lugs can be physically manipulated before building to form almost any desired angle.

All lugs are generally made of mild steel, a malleable form of steel which contains a low percentage of carbon. Head and seat lugs are usually made by stamping and forming two separate parts, which are welded together. Bottom bracket shells can be made in similar fashion, with a welded seam, or they can be cast. Either method forms an acceptable product. Fork crowns may be cast, stamped, or forged. They are usually made of mild steel, but some crowns employ chrome molybdenum steel for extra strength. Stamped plate crowns are usually found on less expensive frames. The style of the lugs—whether they are filigreed or plain, ornate or cut away—is a matter of personal preferance. The more ornate lug styles require more work for proper execution, and therefore cost much more. Cut-away lugs can reduce the weight of the bike to a small degree, but the weight advantage gained is more psychological than physical. This is not to say that it is unimportant. A racer who believes that his bike is the lightest may be more successful because of his belief in the superiority of his bike.

On a majority of mass-produced frames, the lugs are used just as they are received from the manufacturer. They have thick, rough contours and irregular edges. The irregularities persist and are often increased in the rapid production brazing process, and are very clearly present in the finished product.

As the quality of a frame increases, the lugs become more and more meticulously prepared and finished. The contours and edges of the lugs become even and thin, so that on a fine frame, at the lug perimeter, there is a smooth transition to the round shape of the tube, giving the joint a completely unified appearance. A fine lug will show no evidence of weld marks or parting lines from casting or forging; these are all filed away by the master frame builder. In some cases, the lugs are cut in elaborate patterns, as mentioned above, for lightness and decorative beauty.

In the construction of all fine frames, the finish, including the paint or plating, will attempt to show and preserve the quality of the metal finishing work that was done beforehand.

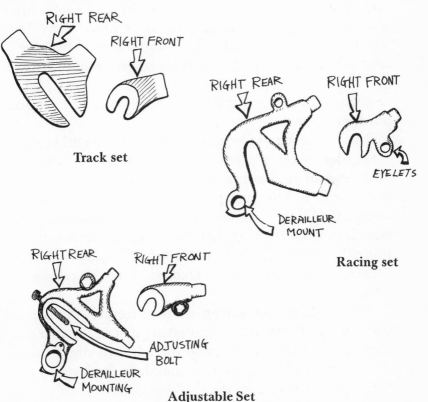

RIGHT REAR

RIGHT FRONT

Track set

RIGHT REAR

RIGHT FRONT

EYELETS

DERAILLEUR MOUNT

Racing set

RIGHT REAR

RIGHT FRONT

ADJUSTING BOLT

DERAILLEUR MOUNTING

Adjustable Set

FORK ENDS AND OTHER FIXTURES

The fork ends are flat plates of mild steel with U shaped slots for the wheel axles. They are either forged or stamped to their shape, and are then brazed into pre-cut slots at the ends of the chain stays, the seat stays, and the fork blades. They can be built with mounting brackets for gear changers, or they can have eyelets for the mounting of fender braces or luggage racks.

The most common set of fork ends used on quality frames is the type with adjusting screws for changing the position of the rear wheel. The adjustability attained is of questionable value; moving the wheel forward or back can change the chain length, but this should be taken care of when the bicycle is being assembled, either by sprocket changes, adding or subtracting links of the chain, or changer adjustment. If a frame builder has built a bike with chain stays of unequal length, or if the wheel is improperly dished, the wheel can be positioned to correct the error, but in either case the result will not be a "true" or aligned product.

The racing set pictured is designed for rapid replacement of wheels. It is simple and trouble free, having no screws to get bent or stripped, and no springs to break or lose. The only problem that might occur in using the racing set as an alternative to the more common adjustable type is that the plates are thinner; this calls for the tightening of a wheel's quick release skewer before the wheel is clamped into the racing fork end.

Fork ends for track frames are extremely simple and sturdy. There are no mounting places for gear changers and accessories, and the tabs are larger than those for other bikes to accommodate the larger diameter stays used in track frame construction.

Less expensive frames are equipped with nondescript stamped fork ends. These are usually made of thin material, and have no provision for mounting even a gear changer.

There are miscellaneous special fittings other than the lugs and fork ends which are sometimes brazed on a frame for the mounting of carrier racks, pumps, lamps, water bottles, and shifting mechanisms. Guides for brake and gear cables are also brazed to some frames. These fittings are often brazed to the frame tubes in places other than where the tubes are butted to adequate thickness. The brazing in such cases does affect the strength of the tubes, and can increase the likelihood of tube failure at the affected points. This is more of a problem on light tube frames than on the heavier models. The problem can be minimized by using low temperature silver alloy filler for the application of such fittings, instead of common brass alloy.

DESIGN

In many respects, the design of bicycle frames has not progressed significantly since the early 1900s. A simple diamond and double triangle design was used then as it is used now, and the construction methods were similar, employing thin steel tubes and lugs, and brazing or welding them together. The wheelbases of early frames were relatively long, and the head and seat angles were shallow (making the tubes farther from vertical than on modern bikes), and relatively poor metallurgy necessitated heavier frames. But as the quality of the steel available improved, and as butted tubes came into use, the weight decreased. The angles became more upright on track frames, and later, as roads improved, on road bike frames. Other than those developments, though, bicycle frames have all stayed within fairly close limits of design. Unusual innovations which were tried from time to time never lasted, because the basic design has always proven to be more efficient.

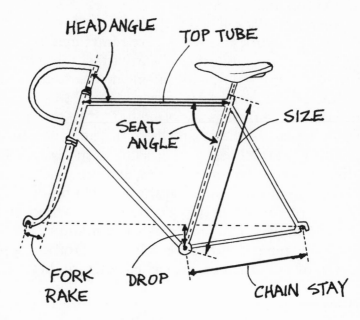

There are only seven measurements that are critical in frame design; all other measurements follow necessarily. The seven are shown in the deceptively simple diagram. They are: frame size (or seat tube length), top tube length, chain stay length, head angle, seat angle, drop, and fork rake. In any discussion of design, one must remember that *all* of the seven act together to make a composite result.

Many different methods are used to calculate the proper frame size or seat tube length for a rider. There is usually about one inch of leeway in the frame size which will be acceptable for a given body size. As a general rule, though, Americans tend to get frames more than an inch too large for their body size, expressing an age-old tendency to get the biggest material possession they can for the money. Biggest car, biggest house, biggest bike frame. Thus it is common to see people riding bikes with 25 inch frames, when they would be much more comfortable and efficient on a 23 inch frame.

Frame size is measured from the center of the bottom bracket axle to the top of the seat lug. Some builders make the measurement to the imaginary point where the axes or center lines of the top and seat tubes meet. Their frames are approximately one and a half centimeters larger than frames with the same size numbers made by other frame builders.

SIZE CHART

LEG LENGTH	FRAME SIZE	TOP TUBE	SEAT HEIGHT (to top)
79–80	48.5–49.5	50.5–52.0	13.5
81–82	50.0–51.0	51.5–53.5	14.0
83–84	51.5–52.5	53.0–54.0	14.5
85–86	53.0–54.0	54.0–55.0	15.0
87–88	54.5–55.5	54.5–55.5	15.5
89–90	56.0–57.0	55.5–56.5	16.0
91–92	57.5–58.5	57.5–58.5	16.5
93–94	59.0–60.0	58.5–59.0	17.0
95–96	60.5–61.5	59.0–59.5	17.5
97–98	62.0–63.0	59.5	18.0
99–100	63.5–64.5	60.0	18.5
101–102	65.0–66.0	60.5	19.0

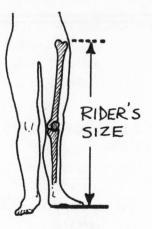

Italian method of measuring

The diagram and table shown can be used to form a general idea of what frame size, top tube length, and seat height a rider needs. It is not foolproof, and does not take into account such variables as unusual body proportions, peculiar riding styles, or unorthodox riding positions. But it is usable for the determination of an approximate frame size. For the equivalent measurements in inches, use the conversion table in the appendix.

If you want to have a frame custom made, it is smartest to have the builder measure you himself, so he can use his own formula to fit you with exactly the right size frame.

To arrive at a precise idea of the *largest* frame you can use, lie on the floor and angle your feet at 45 degrees so that the balls of your feet are pressing against a wall, as shown. Measure the distance from your crotch to the wall. Add three quarters of an inch for the thickness of your pedals. From the total, subtract first the length of your crank (usually between 165 and 175 mm, or six and a half to seven inches),

146

then the height of the top of your seat above the frame (at least 6.3 cm or two and a half inches). The resulting measurement will be absolutely the largest frame you can possibly ride. Normally you will want a frame that is two to four inches shorter than that.

Within limits, a tourist will tend to ride a bike frame closer to the largest possible, so that he can ride with the handlebars in a high, easily reached position. Since it is ill advised from a mechanical point of view to have the stem protruding more than two inches out of the top of the headset, it is necessary to enlarge the frame to accommodate the higher handlebar position.

Track racers usually prefer a frame somewhat smaller than that which they would use for road racing. The smaller frame, coupled with special slanted stems and deep drop handlebars, allows the racer to have an extremely low handlebar position, which is better suited for track events.

The distance between the handlebars and the seat is a function of the length of the stem extension and

WALL

Al's method of measuring

RIDER'S SIZE

45°∠

FLOOR

the length of the top tube. Top tube length varies by as much as one and a half inches from builder to builder. It is one of the lengths that affect the overall balance of the rider's weight on the frame. A 45% front and 55% rear wheel weight ratio is the goal of the builder, but the balance cannot be achieved by lengthening or shortening the top tube alone. If the top tube is too long, the bike may develop speed wobble or "shimmy" at high velocity. If the tube is too short, the bicycle's pedals will hit the front wheel.

The angles, the fork rake, and the chain stay length of any frame are the most important factors in determining a finished bike's stiffness or limberness, its stability and energy absorbing properties.

The head angle and the fork rake function together and affect the handling and shock abosrbing properties of the front part of the frame. The head angle generally falls between 72 and 75 degrees. The fork rake varies between one inch and two and three-quarters inches. A short rake combined with a steep (or greater) head angle make for extremely positive, quick handling, but the combination gives a harsh ride on anything but smooth pavement. It is normally reserved for track bike frames. A shallow or lesser head angle, like 72 degrees, coupled with a fork rake of two and a half inches, may be found on touring bikes, especially those designed to carry heavy luggage.

Seat angle affects the position of the saddle over the hanger (bottom bracket), and therefore the distribution of the rider's weight on the frame. The angle is usually the same as the head angle, or slightly less steep. To get a reasonably accurate idea of what seat angle a bike has, get a metric ruler and measure the distance from the axes of the seat and top tubes (A) to the point (B) along the top tube that is directly above the center of the bottom bracket axle. Put the bike on a level surface and use a plumb line or weighted string to find point B. Then find the angle on the chart on the next page.

Chain stay length affects the weight distribution of the rider by changing the position of the rear wheel in relation to the rest of the bike. It also affects the energy absorbing properties of a frame. The stay is measured from the center of the rear wheel axle to the center of the bottom bracket axle, and can be as short as sixteen inches, or as long as eighteen inches in rare cases. A shorter chain stay will produce a frame that is very responsive, one that wastes little of the rider's energy by flexing side to side, or "whipping." But as with steep angles and short fork rake, the short chain stay causes a frame to be stiff to the point where some consider it too harsh.

Ideally, a frame should be stiff enough to transmit all energy applied on the pedals to the rear wheel, yet flexible enough to absorb all road shocks. For touring under normal conditions, a frame built of light tubing is in order, with 72 degree head and seat angles, a two

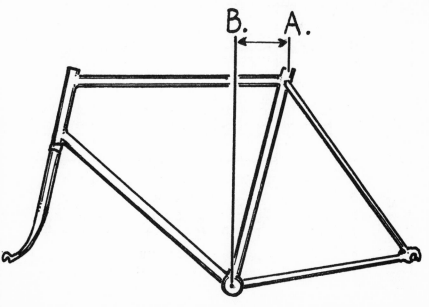

SEAT ANGLE CHART

Size of Bike (in centimeters)	SEAT ANGLE					
	72°	72°30'	73°	73°30'	74°	74°30'
	DISTANCE A — B					
55.0	17.0	16.5	16.0	15.6	15.2	14.7
55.5	17.1	16.7	16.2	15.8	15.3	14.8
56.0	17.3	16.8	16.4	15.9	15.4	14.9
56.5	17.5	17.0	16.5	16.0	15.6	15.0
57.0	17.6	17.1	16.7	16.2	15.7	15.2
57.5	17.8	17.3	16.8	16.3	15.8	15.4
58.0	17.9	17.4	17.0	16.4	16.0	15.5
58.5	18.1	17.6	17.1	16.6	16.1	15.6
59.0	18.2	17.7	17.2	16.7	16.3	15.8
59.5	18.4	17.9	17.4	16.9	16.4	15.9
60.0	18.5	18.0	17.5	17.0	16.5	16.0
60.5	18.7	18.2	17.7	17.2	16.7	16.2
61.0	18.9	18.3	17.8	17.3	16.8	16.3
61.5	19.0	18.5	18.0	17.4	16.9	16.4
62.0	19.2	18.6	18.1	17.6	17.1	16.5

inch fork rake and seventeen inch chain stays. The bike made with that design will be comfortable and easy to ride. It won't be exceptionally responsive, but under the conditions of its use it will be entirely adequate.

As more weight is added to a bike, as in touring with a large amount of equipment, it becomes necessary to strengthen the frame tubing, extend the fork rake to as far as two and three-quarters inches, and increase the chain stay length to as much as seventeen and a half inches. But variations in frame design alone cannot accommodate the weight. Provision should be made to carry the load low on the frame, and the weight should be distributed as evenly as possible over the front and back wheels. If all of the load is added to the rear wheel, there will be a tendency for the front wheel to float and produce speed wobble. If all the weight is added to the front of the bike, it becomes almost impossible to steer and balance effectively.

As the usage of a bike frame tends more and more towards high speed riding with no extra weight, more upright head angles are in order. Some road racing bikes are now available with the following measurements: head angles of 74 degrees, 30 minutes, four centimeter or one and nine-sixteenths inches rake in the fork, and chain stays measuring sixteen and three-eighths inches or less. These dimensions would once have been considered appropriate only on a track frame, but with smooth road surfaces and resilient butted frame tubing, they are flexible enough to make an acceptable criterium or smooth road racing frame. The handling is quick and positive, and the frame absorbs very little energy. A frame with those dimensions and angles might prove too responsive for the average slower-paced rider or tourist, though he might become accustomed to the bike's handling in time.

There is a lot of confusion in general about the terms "stiff" and "flexible" as they are used to describe bike frames. For one thing, a frame which seems positive and quick-handling to one rider may seem harsh and skitterish to another rider. A frame which seems limber and resilient to one may seem soft and lifeless to another. The terms are subjective; personal preference controls their meaning. In determining whether a frame is stiff or limber, the wheel-base is sometimes used as a guide; shorter frames are often stiffer, longer frames are considered more flexible. But the wheel-base on any bike is only a result of a number of other dimensions of the frame. It is possible to design frames with identical wheelbases, but with great variations in all of the component measurements, and therefore great differences in stiffness, handling, and weight distribution. So wheelbase alone can't be used to determine a bike's design.

Another device for guessing stiffness which might be misleading is gauging the clearances between the tires and the frame. The clearances are partly a function of the size of tires used, the type of brakes used, and whether fenders are used or not. None of these factors has a great effect on the handling of the bike, so judgments should not be made in terms of clearances, but in terms of the seven critical measurements.

One clearance problem often cited is that of the front wheel and the toe clip. On frames which have upright head angles, short top tubes, and small fork rake, the toe clip will hit the front wheel when the pedal is in its frontmost position and the fork is turned towards the pedal. This circumstance may on the surface seem to be a defect in frame design, but under most riding conditions it will be no problem. The toe clip and wheel will only collide if the bike is being ridden very slowly, through sharp turns.

Although the seat stays are less significant than the other frame elements in determining the bike's stiffness, they still play a role in the overall product. The size and gauge of the stay tubes can affect the overall rigidity of a frame somewhat. This is more important if the frame is carrying a great deal of weight, or if it is being used under great amounts of stress, as in sprinting. There are several different methods of attaching seat stays to the seat lugs, to the seat tube below the lug, to the seat itself, or to the seat tube and the top tube together. Generally, the more upright the angle of the seat stay for any given size of frame, the stiffer the back of the frame will be. Since the stresses concentrated at the joint of the top of the seat stay and the rest of the frame are minimal, many individualistic and decorative methods of attachment are employed.

Drop is the distance that the center of the bottom bracket axle is below an imaginary horizontal line drawn between the centers of the two wheel axles. It is not an element of design that obviously affects a bike's handling, but it can be tactically significant in races. The drop of a finished bike can be measured by subtracting the height of the center of the bottom bracket over level ground from the height of the center of the wheels. This measuring method can be made inaccurate by any irregularity of the ground surface, or by the use of different wheels or tires, so builders usually prefer making direct drop measurements with a string between the wheel axles.

The drop should be as low as possible, but not so low that the pedals hit the ground. The lower the drop is, the lower the center of gravity of the bike will be, which can improve handling, and a quality which can't be described, but which many riders claim exists, namely "roll" or rolling resistance. A frame with a lower hanger seems to have superior ease in moving when compared to a similar bike with a high hanger. From a practical point of view, a normal road bike equipped with 680 mm tubular tires and 170 mm cranks can have a drop no greater than 8.2 cm. If the crank length is to be increased, the drop must be correspondingly decreased to retain pedal clearance above the road. If the rider intends to be pedaling at high speed through corners, as in criterium racing, it becomes necessary to decrease the drop significantly, to six cm, or in some instances, perhaps even five cm. International racing regulations limit the drop to a minimum of four cm.

High drop may sometimes be used on bikes built for long, fast downhill runs, so that the rider can pedal around fast curves. Cyclo cross bikes also employ a high drop, for clearance over obstacles. A high hanger is of great importance in sprint track racing as well. While maneuvering up and down track banking, or while riding slowly as in sprint stalling tactics, on a steeply banked track, it is necessary to have a high hanger to prevent the pedals from striking the track. On the other hand, a pursuit track bike frame does not require the same high hanger, since the rider stays in the pole position at all times while moving at a constant rate of speed.

ALIGNMENT

A bicycle frame should be received by a customer in perfect alignment. This means:

1. The axes (center lines) of the four main frame tubes should be in the same vertical plane.

2. The bottom bracket shell should be perpendicular to the frame plane.

3. The rear fork ends should be equidistant from the frame plane, and an axle placed in the ends should be perpendicular to the frame plane. The distance

between the fork end plates should be equal to the width of a wheel hub.

4. The front fork should have blades of equal length. The axis of the fork crown should be parallel to an axle placed in the fork ends. The fork end plates should be parallel to each other and equidistant from the center plane of the fork. The straight upper section of each fork blade should be in line with the fork steering column.

Some of these limits can be checked easily by eye or by the use of adjustable caliper dividers, a straight edge, and a length of string. A quality frame should pass all the tests for alignment perfectly. Any variation should have been corrected during construction.

The frame plane alignment can be checked by sighting past the head tube, from directly in front of it, to the seat tube, which should be exactly parallel right behind it.

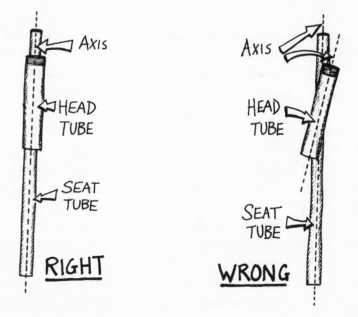

AXIS
HEAD TUBE
SEAT TUBE
RIGHT

AXIS
HEAD TUBE
SEAT TUBE
WRONG

Hanger or bottom bracket alignment can be checked after the cranks have been installed. As a crank goes around, the distances from the tip of the crank to the sides of the seat and down tubes should be equal.

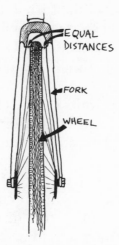

To check the placement of the fork ends, slide wheels in and out of them. It should be easy to do without any adjustments to wheel or fork. When the wheel is set properly in either the front or the back fork ends, the tire should be equidistant from the two fork blades, or seat and chain stays, assuming that the wheels and tires are properly trued. If the bicycle is stood up perfectly straight, with the front wheel steering straight ahead, you should be able to sight along the profile of the tires, from behind, and see that they are perfectly in line. This test is done most easily if someone is riding the bike in a straight line away from you.

To check a front fork, you can remove it from the headset, and stand it up with the tips on a flat surface. A weighted string hanging from a point along the axis of the steering tube should fall perpendicular to the flat surface, equidistant from the fork end plates. If you hold the fork horizontally and sight along it from the top of the steering column, the leading edges of the crown should be parallel to the leading edges of the fork tips. From the side, the blades should be in line with the axis of the steering column.

Chainstay alignment can be checked by tying a string to one of the rear fork ends, and running it

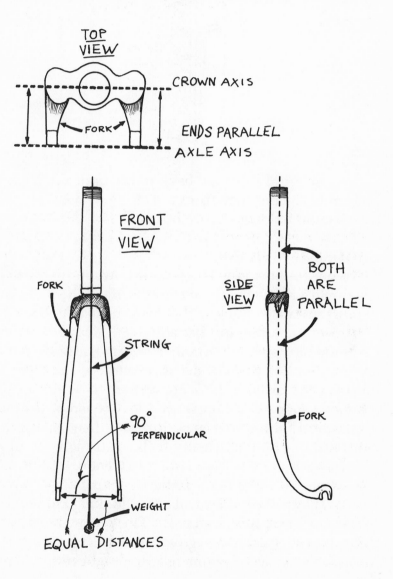

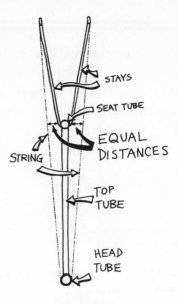

around the head tube and back to the opposite rear
fork end. The distance from the string to the seat
tube should be the same on both sides of the frame.

CHOOSING A FRAME

No matter how much a cyclist knows about frames,
or no matter how much he can *say* about them, he is
in most instances stuck with what is available. Each
builder or manufacturer has a definite idea as to what
the best solution to the frame problem is. His designs
are the result of years of design evolution, and have
been proven, as far as he is concerned, to be the most
workable. Once a builder settles on a design, it is more
economical for him to repeat it rather than change it
constantly. A builder usually feels so strongly about
his designs that even if you are lucky enough to have
him accept an order for a particular frame of your own
design, the final product will arrive looking as if the
builder had designed it after all. This seems to be a
result partly of personal ego and partly of good sense.
Most frame angles and dimensions have been tried at

one time or another. The broader the background of the builder, the more likely he is to know the effects of unusual frame designs. He will not want to build a bike that might hurt his reputation by producing a poor ride. Nor will any builder who is proud of his design want to build a frame that looks as if it was designed by one of his competitors. If you want to insist on a particular design, go to a builder who already uses it to build frames. The whole bicycle experience is expansive enough to allow for personal variations, and expression of almost any knowledgeable preference.

The best procedure for you as a prospective buyer is to check all the various designs and qualities of finish that are available to you. Then try to correlate each design to what you want to do with the bicycle. Almost anything you would want is available if you have the time and patience to wait, and the money to pay for a good frame. There are even a few frame builders who will accept your frame designs. Generally, though, if you decide to get a custom frame, it is best to tell the builder what you are planning to do with it, then have him measure you by his own method of measuring, and design the frame to fit your needs.

FEELINGS

The feeling of a frame is difficult to explain. It is partly aesthetic, partly kinetic, and partly psychological. A rider may ride faster on a frame because the world champion rides on a similar frame, or because someone whose opinion he respects considers it a better frame. He might even react to the actual design of the frame. On an uneven road surface, a frame might feel springy and lively, and the rider might respond by riding accordingly. On a rapid descent, a frame might feel extremely solid and stable; the rider will ride faster than he would on another frame, even if he doesn't actually have better control. He rides faster because he feels more secure.

At the other extreme of feeling, a frame might be solid to the point that it creates a sensation of "flying" over rough road surfaces. This feeling might make the rider think that he is out of control, even though he probably is not at all. Or a rider might be constantly aware of a supposed defect in either the design or execution of his frame; this will make him slower and less secure as he rides, even if the defect in no way affects the physical performance of the frame.

For maximum satisfaction, a rider should learn limits within which he will accept a frame design. Then he should find a frame that most closely approximates his ideal within those limits, purchase it, and thoroughly accustom himself to the individual peculiarities of the bike. Accustoming oneself to a frame takes time even for an experienced rider. After the first period of enjoyment of a new bike, there is always a period of adjustments of both the bike and the rider, as the rider familiarizes himself with the frame. It is not a good idea for a racer to get a new frame in the middle of a season, or for a tourist to start a cross-continental trip on a new frame. It is necessary to ride a bike enough to know all of its handling idiosyncrasies before using it for competition or a long ride.

The whole idea is to become so much a part of your bike that you don't even think about it while you are riding. All your mental energy while riding should be directed toward the event in which you are participating—either competing in a race, experiencing a new area you are traveling through, or enjoying the company of the people you are riding with. The bicycle, in other words, is best used as a vehicle for a certain experience, as well as a vehicle of transportation. The bicycle's frame design *as a whole unit* should make the experience as good as possible, and never be considered an end in itself. Bicycles are not built to be used as status symbols. The cyclist should *ride* his chosen bike, instead of bull-shitting about its angles or its chain stay length.

ADDRESSES

AMERICAN BICYCLE LEAGUE OF AMERICA
(racing association)
Alfred J. Toefield, President
87-66—256th Street
Floral Park, Long Island, New York 11001

Frank Small, Secretary
4233—205th Street
Bayside, Long Island, New York 11361

AMERICAN YOUTH HOSTELS INC. (AYH)
20 West 17th Street
New York, New York 10011

BOOKS ABOUT CYCLING (store and mail order)
P.O. Box 208
Nevada City, California 95959

CATALOGUES AND MAIL ORDER HOUSES
Big Wheel Ltd.
340 Holly Street
Denver, Colorado 80220

Cupertino Bike Shop
10080 Randy Lane
Cupertino, California 95014

Cyclopedia (Gene Portuesi)
311 North Mitchell Street
Cadillac, Michigan 49601

Chuck Harris (rear view mini-mirror)
Beech Hill
Warren, New Hampshire

LEAGUE OF AMERICAN WHEELMEN (club)
5118 Foster Avenue
Chicago, Illinois 60630

LOCK STATISTICS
John O. Dierking's Study on Bicycle Locks
Mechanical Engineering, Design Division
Stanford University
Stanford, California 94026

MAGAZINES
Bicycling
256 Sutter Street
San Francisco, California 94108

Bike World
95 Main Street
Los Altos, California 94022

Le Cycliste
18, Rue du Commandeur
19, Rue Montbrun
Paris 14^e, France

U.S. GEOLOGICAL SURVEY (topographical maps)
Distribution Section
U.S. Geological Survey
1200 South Eads Street
Arlington, Virginia 22202
OR
Distribution Section
U.S. Geological Survey
Federal Center
Denver, Colorado 80225

APPENDIX

BRITISH STANDARD WIRE GAUGE

S.W. Gauge	Thickness	
	Inches	mm
10	0.128	3.2512
11	0.116	2.9464
12	0.104	2.6416
13	0.092	2.3368
14	0.080	2.0320
15	0.072	1.8288
16	0.064	1.6256
17	0.056	1.4224
18	0.048	1.2192
19	0.040	1.0160
20	0.036	0.9144
21	0.032	0.8128
22	0.028	0.7112
23	0.024	0.6096
24	0.022	0.5588
25	0.020	0.5080

CONVERSION TABLE

Inches		mm	Inches		mm
1/32	.03125	.7937	1-3/8	1.37500	34.9250
1/16	.06250	1.5875	1-1/2	1.50000	38.1000
3/32	.09375	2.3812	1-19/32	1.59375	40.4812
	.11600	2.9464	1-5/8	1.62500	41.2750
1/8	.12500	3.1750	1-3/4	1.75000	44.4500
5/32	.15625	3.9687	1-7/8	1.87500	47.6250
3/16	.18750	4.7625	2	2.00000	50.8000
7/32	.21875	5.5562		2.10000	53.3400
1/4	.25000	6.3500		2.20000	55.8800
9/32	.28125	7.1437	2-1/4	2.25000	57.1500
5/16	.31250	7.9375		2.30000	58.4200
11/32	.34375	8.7312		2.35000	59.6900
3/8	.37500	9.5250		2.40000	60.9600
13/32	.40625	10.3187		2.45000	62.2300
7/16	.43750	11.1125	2-1/2	2.50000	63.5000
15/32	.46875	11.9062	2-3/4	2.75000	69.8500
1/2	.50000	12.7000	3	3.00000	76.2000
17/32	.53125	13.4937	3-1/4	3.25000	82.5500
9/16	.56250	14.2875	3-1/2	3.50000	88.9000
	.56600	14.3764	3-3/4	3.75000	95.2500
19/32	.59375	15.0812	4	4.00000	101.6000
5/8	.62500	15.8750	4-1/4	4.25000	107.9500
21/32	.65625	16.6687	4-1/2	4.50000	114.3000
11/16	.68750	17.4625	4-3/4	4.75000	120.6500
23/32	.71875	18.2562	5	5.00000	127.0000
3/4	.75000	19.0500	5-1/4	5.25000	133.3500
25/32	.78125	19.8437	5-1/2	5.50000	139.7000
13/16	.81250	20.6375	5-3/4	5.75000	146.0500
27/32	.84375	21.4312	6	6.00000	152.4000
7/8	.87500	22.2250	6-1/4	6.25000	158.7500
29/32	.90625	23.0187	6-1/2	6.50000	165.1000
15/16	.93750	23.8125	6-3/4	6.75000	171.4500
31/32	.96875	24.6062	7	7.00000	177.8000
1 inch	1.00000	25.4000	For larger numbers, move		
1-1/8	1.12500	28.5750	decimals to the right;		
1-1/4	1.25000	31.7500	e.g. 24 inches = 609.6 mm		

GEAR TABLE (27 Inch Wheel)

CHAINWHEEL TEETH

Rear Sprocket	40	42	44	46	48	50	52
13	83.1"	87.2"	91.4"	95.5"	99.7"	103.8"	108.0"
14	77.1	81.0	84.8	88.7	92.6	96.4	100.3
15	72.0	75.6	79.2	82.8	86.4	90.0	93.6
16	67.5	70.9	74.2	77.6	81.0	84.3	87.7
17	63.5	66.7	69.9	73.0	76.2	79.4	82.6
18	60.0	63.0	66.0	69.0	72.0	75.0	78.0
19	56.8	59.7	62.5	65.4	68.2	71.2	73.9
20	54.0	56.7	59.4	62.1	64.8	67.5	70.2
21	51.4	54.0	56.6	59.1	61.7	64.3	66.8
22	49.1	51.5	54.0	56.4	58.9	61.3	63.8
23	47.0	49.3	51.6	54.0	56.3	58.6	61.0
24	45.0	47.2	49.5	51.7	54.0	56.2	58.5
25	43.2	45.4	47.5	49.7	51.8	54.0	56.2
26	41.6	43.6	45.7	47.8	49.8	51.9	54.0
28	38.6	40.5	42.4	44.3	46.3	48.2	50.1

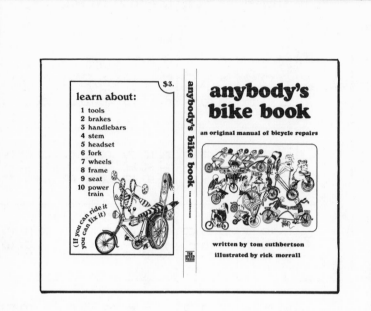

INDEX

A

Abrasions 70
Aching bottom 73
Airplanes 48
Alignment (frame) 154
Angles (frame) 148
Animals, dealing with
  38–42
Ankling 110

B

Bachrach, Burt 54
Backache 73
Basic biking law 21
Beach riding 119
Beginners, lessons for 1
Bleeding 72
Boils 72
Bottom, aching 73
Brakes, checking 28
  quality 12, 16
Braking technique
  2, 65, 67, 113, 123
Brazing (frames) 135
Broken limbs 70
Bumper-type carrier 50
Buses 32, 46
Butting 128

C

Camping 60, 115
Carriers, bike 49–56
Car-top carrier 53
Cattle guards, crossing 36
Chain, lubricating 30
Choosing a bike 4
Cold weather riding 72, 74
Collapsible bikes 6
Commuting routes 87
Cranks, cotterless 13
Curves 70
Custom bikes, buying
  8, 14, 140
Cuts 70
Cycle camping 115
Cyclo cross 121

D

Derailleur adjustment 30
  quality 12, 18
  shifting 2, 65, 67
Design (frame) 143
Dirt road riding 120
Dogs 38–41
Drop (frame) 153

E

Elements, dealing with 74

F

Fanatics, trips for 111
First aid 60, 70–73
Fork ends 10, 142
Fold-up bikes 6, 46
Four and five speeds 6–7
  Alignment 154

169

Frame, brazing 134
  design 143
  drop 144, 153
  failure 139
  finish 140
  fork ends 141
  general 125–161
  joint bonding 134
  size 7, 11, 145
  stiff vs. limber 14
  trueness 12, 14, 17, 154
  tubes 126–134
Freeways 42
French armband light 24

G
Gandhi 40
Gears, inches 17
  quality 12
  progression 16
  range 16, 115
  shifting technique 2
Gun nuts 42

H
Handlebar position 18, 65
  stem 29
Head injuries 70
Heat exhaustion 72
Heatstroke 72
Highways 42
High wheeler 111
Hot-rodders 42
How many should ride? 61
Hunters 42, 121

I
Ice riding 119
Intersections 32
Intervals 106

J
"Jump" 108

K
Kaiser, Al 111
Katabalic breezes 79
Keep to the right 32, 37

L
Laws 20–26, 34
Learning to ride 1
Lights 23
Limited access roads 42
Living on a bike 115
Local bike routes 85
Locks 6, 13, 19
Lugs (frame) 134

M
Mandrel 128
Maps 42, 85–101
Measures (metric and
  inches) 165
Moulton four speed 6
Mountain breezes 79

N
Night riding 22–24

O

Off-shore on-shore breezes 80
One speed bikes 5
Ordinary 111

P

Pace 66
Packing bikes for shipment 46
Pedals 30
Pedaling technique 65, 70
Penny-farthing 111
Picking a bike 4
Pimples 72
Pressure (tire) 27
Prevailing winds 74
Public transportation 44—48

R

Railroad tracks 35, 36
Rain 74
Raleigh Superbe 6
Restoring a high wheeler 111
Right side, riding on 32, 37
Rims 69
Road racing 106
Rollers 108
Routes, commuting 87
    country escape 95
    local 85
    touring 101

S

Safe bike 26—30
Safety, for beginners 2—3
    general 20—43
Seat position 7, 11, 18, 65
Seatpost 29
Shifting gears 2
Side of street to ride on 32, 37
Sitting in 79
Size (of bike) 7, 11, 145
Skyways 42
Slatted storm drains 35
Solo cycling 61
Spare tire 59
Speed, danger of 36
Spokes 15
Stiff vs. limber (frame) 14, 152
Storm drains 35
Super highways 42
Superbe, Raleigh 6

T

Tar 37
Ten speed bikes, buying 8—19
    gear ranges 16—18
    shifting 2
Three speeds, buying 5
Tires, 12, 27, 67
Toll roads 42
Tools 59
Toter 50
Touring trips 101
Tracks, crossing 35, 36

Traffic, avoiding
31, 36, 86, 95
dealing with 20—32
Trailer (car) 58
Trains 45
Training wheels 1
Transportation, bikes
5, 44—55
public 44
Trashmo 5, 118
Trips, commuting 87
country escape 95
for fanatics 111
local 85
touring 101
Trueness (frame)
12, 14, 17, 154
Tubes (frame) 126—134

V

Valley breezes 79
Vehicle codes 20—26
Veloce 66

W

Water bottle 59
Weight distribution 148
Welding (frame) 134
Wet roads 37
Wise riding style 64
Wheels, buying 15, 115
checking 27
When to ride 62, 74
Wind 75—80
Winter training 108

Author on a high wheeler (or "penny-farthing" bike)